Shared Experience, Notting...
and West Yorkshire Playhou...
in association with Oxford P...

World Premiere

C000129309

Mary
Shelley

By Helen Edmundson

SHARED EXPERIENCE

Nottingham Playhouse

WY PLAY HOUSE

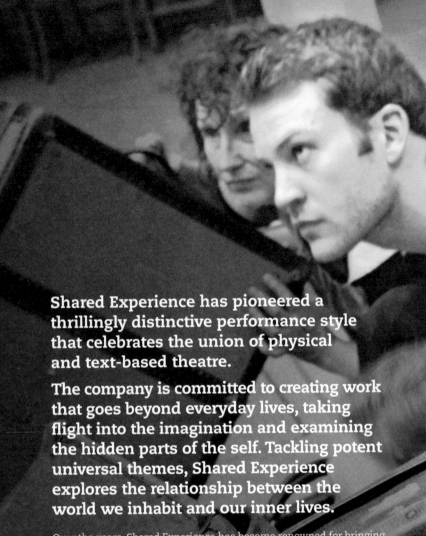

Shared Experience has pioneered a thrillingly distinctive performance style that celebrates the union of physical and text-based theatre.

The company is committed to creating work that goes beyond everyday lives, taking flight into the imagination and examining the hidden parts of the self. Tackling potent universal themes, Shared Experience explores the relationship between the world we inhabit and our inner lives.

Over the years, Shared Experience has become renowned for bringing literary classics to life in bold, imaginative ways. **Nottingham Playhouse** and **West Yorkshire Playhouse** are two of the leading producing theatres in the UK, with dynamic reputations for bringing the best new drama to audiences nationwide.

Following the success of their collaboration on *Caucasian Chalk Circle* in 2009, all three partners reunited to begin development work on *Mary Shelley* as part of West Yorkshire Playhouse's *Transform 2011* Festival. The result is this ambitious production which places the life of an extraordinary woman centre stage.

Photo: Naomi Dawson

SHARED
EXPERIENCE

The Company

Mary	Kristin Atherton
William Godwin	William Chubb
Percy Bysshe Shelley	Ben Lamb
Fanny Godwin	Flora Nicholson
Mrs Godwin	Sadie Shimmin
Jane Clairmont	Shannon Tarbet

Other parts played by members of the company

Writer	Helen Edmundson
Director	Polly Teale
Designer	Naomi Dawson
Composer	Keith Clouston
Movement Director	Liz Ranken
Lighting Designer	Chris Davey
Sound Designer	Drew Baumohl
Production Managers	Eddie de Pledge, Jasper Gilbert and Sam Paterson
Deputy Stage Manager	Lauren Harvey
West Yorkshire Playhouse SM	Julie Issott
West Yorkshire Playhouse ASM	Kirsty Louise Airlie
Nottingham Playhouse CSM	Jane Eliot-Webb
Nottingham Playhouse ASM	Stuart Lambert
Touring Company Stage Manager	Matthew Hales
Touring Assistant Stage Manager	Natasha Emma Jones
Touring Sound Engineer	Drew Baumohl
Voice	Majella Hurley
Casting Director	Amy Ball
Assistant Director	Cecily Boys
Relighters	Will Evans and Andrew Ellis
Mary Shelley Resource Pack	Kate Saxon, Aisling Zambon and Aoibheann Kelly

The performance will last approximately 2 hrs and 45 mins including an interval.

First performed in the Courtyard Theatre, West Yorkshire Playhouse on Friday 16 March 2012.

The set, props and costumes for this production were created by the West Yorkshire Playhouse Workshops.

This play began with a question: how did Mary Shelley, aged only eighteen, come to write a novel of such weight and power as *Frankenstein*? I knew the story of the Villa Diodati, and the external impetus for her sitting down to write, but where did the thoughts come from? The themes? For *Frankenstein* is clearly more than a spine-chiller; it is a novel of ideas.

She dedicated the story to her father, William Godwin, the radical political philosopher. Much has been said about Shelley's influence on Mary at this time, (some have even suggested that he had a hand in writing *Frankenstein*), but as I began my research, I quickly discovered that Shelley's own ideas and preoccupations had been inspired to a large degree by Godwinian philosophy. He and Mary shared a passion for her father's work, and I started to understand that it was this passion more than anything, which had equipped her to write so brilliantly about such ideas as the consequences of treating men like beasts.

But there was more. Mary was writing *Frankenstein* at a time when her relationship with her father was under great strain – when he had refused all contact with her for almost two years. The novel is more than a homage to his philosophies; it is a criticism of his nature and his choices, a warning, a reprimand and a huge cry for understanding. It is these elements, I think, which give *Frankenstein* its heartfelt urgency and power. I decided to place this complex relationship at the centre of the play, and to see where it took me.

The research I undertook was enormously absorbing and inspiring. Each of the principal characters could be the subject of a play in their own right. I loved delving into Skinner Street – into Mary's troubled family, patched together from bits and pieces of different relationships, crudely stitched – like the monster himself – into a clumsy, dysfunctional form. I loved discovering her sisters, each of whose fate was so bound up with Mary's, and learning about the daring and vision of Shelley's early socialism. It was a pleasure to imagine these people back to life.

And whilst I felt compelled, (as Mary did), to depict the very real and awful dangers of putting principles before emotional need, I hope I have not painted too harsh a picture of idealism. For there is something courageous, surely, in striving to break new ground in the perilous business of living. In deciding to deal with the pain, the guilt, the disapproval this entails, in the belief and hope that, ultimately, humanity will be the richer for your efforts.

Helen Edmundson
February 2012

'The essence of
love is freedom'

Percy Bysshe Shelley

'How beautiful and calm and free thou wert
In thy young wisdom, when the mortal chain
Of Custom thou didst burst and rend in twain
And walked as free as light the clouds among...'
Percy Bysshe Shelley's dedication to Mary

Photo: Naomi Dawson

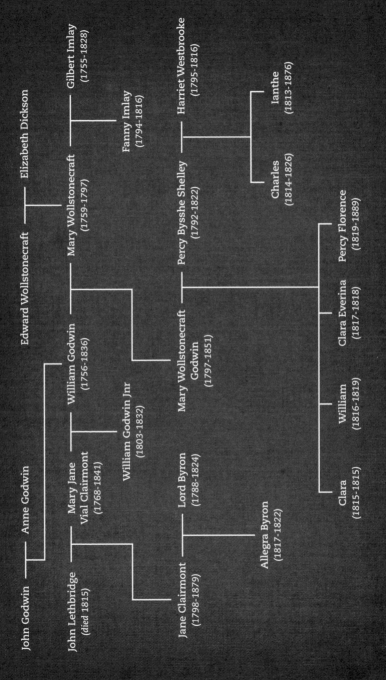

'You had endowed me with perceptions and passions, and then cast me abroad an object for the scorn and horror of mankind'

Mary Shelley's *Frankenstein*

Mary Shelley

by Dr Mark Philp

The wars triggered by the French Revolution in 1789 finally came to a close at the battle of Waterloo in 1815. The initial British response to France's reform of its political order had been warm but it cooled rapidly with the increasing radicalism and violence of the revolution. Fear that the 'French distemper' would spread across the channel resulted in a polarising of political opinion and increasingly repressive activity by the British Government. This lasted for twenty-five years and had a profound effect on British political, literary and cultural life.

Helen Edmundson's play, *Mary Shelley*, focusses on two years (1814-1816), right at the end of this period, in the turbulent lives of six people: Mary Wollstonecraft-Godwin (who became Mary Shelley in 1816 and published *Frankenstein* shortly after these events); her father, the radical philosopher and novelist William Godwin; her step-mother Mary Jane Clairmont; her two step-sisters Fanny Imlay and Jane Clairmont; and the poet Percy Bysshe Shelley. Often hailed as the foremost family of British romanticism, they were also a family of contrasts and tensions: enlightenment and romanticism, reason and imagination, principle and feeling, conformity and rebellion. Those tensions were played out with often tragic consequences in the relationships between Mary Shelley and her family.

Godwin's political philosophy was in part inspired by his positive reaction to the opening events of the French Revolution. His work epitomised enlightenment optimism about the progress of humanity. He believed that through education and the development of the understanding it was possible to foster our innate sense of responsibility, benevolence and goodness. He predicted a future in which virtue would triumph and in which reason would conquer nature, enabling us to achieve immortality. Government may once have been a necessary evil but as mind progressed it would wither away. Authority, law, marriage, contracts, promises – indeed, anything that constrains the sovereignty of the individual's private judgment and freedom to act – would become redundant. His radical vision brought him widespread fame – the essayist William Hazlitt said of him that he 'blazed as a sun in the firmament of reputation; no one was more talked of, more looked up to, more sought after … Truth, moral truth, it was supposed, had here taken up its abode.'

Although Godwin was intellectually radical he was political cautious – wary that precipitate action could produce chaos and delay progress. For the radical John Thelwall, Godwin's 'visionary peculiarities of mind,' which 'recommend the most extensive plan of freedom and innovation ever discussed by any writer in the English language…' were coupled with a conviction that it was necessary 'to reprobate every measure from which even the most moderate reform can rationally be expected.'

'Rise like Lions after slumber
In unvanquishable number –
Shake your chains to earth like dew
Which in sleep had fallen on you –
Ye are many – they are few…
You cannot evict an idea.'
Percy Bysshe Shelley

But for all his caution, Godwin was deeply affected when he fell in love with the feminist writer Mary Wollstonecraft. She was a crucial catalyst in Godwin's life. Their deep and moving relationship, which flourished between April 1796 and September 1797, took the over-rationalist, ex-dissenting minister wholly by surprise. When Wollstonecraft became pregnant they married – not without a certain amount of philosophical embarrassment on Godwin's part. Six months later, Wollstonecraft died following Mary's birth. Stricken with grief, Godwin threw himself into a memoir to commemorate the woman he had loved, not seeing that his work would provide a perfect target for scurrilous attack by the increasingly vituperative reactionary press. From 1798 he was denounced in lecture halls and from pulpits and villified in the loyalist press. He continued to work and write for the next thirty-eight years, producing novels, literary studies, histories and essays, but his reputation never recovered. In 1801 he wrote: 'I have fallen … in one common grave with the cause and love of liberty; and in this sense have been more honoured and illustrated in my decline than ever I was at the tide of my success.'

Godwin was left caring for Mary and for Wollstonecraft's three-year-old daughter Fanny, the child of Wollstonecraft's affair in Paris with Captain Gilbert Imlay. Godwin felt Wollstonecraft's loss acutely. His sister Hannah and his housekeeper, Louisa Jones, cared for the girls while Godwin wrote but he played a central role in the girls' life. Both girls referred to him as Papa, and their relationship with him was warm and affectionate, even if he was often distracted by intellectual concerns.

In December 1801 Godwin married Mary Jane Clairmont. She already had two children, Charles (then 6) and Jane (then 3). The couple's only child, William, was born in 1803. They established a children's publisher and bookshop and produced several works of lasting value, such as Charles and Mary Lamb's *Tales from Shakespeare* (1807). Godwin was not, however, a good manager. Following advice, he tried to increase the capital of the business but this led to one round of borrowing after another – exhausting his credit and his remaining reputation with his friends and former associates. The business struggled for twenty years before being declared bankrupt in 1825.

For much of this time his relationship with Mary Jane was a strained one. She resented his old friends whom she saw as hangers on, and was oppressed by the debts, the work, and Godwin's often very poor health. Their life presented a sharp contrast to the one Godwin had sketched in his philosophical work and in his memoir of Wollstonecraft. These contrasts were obvious to his remaining friends and acquaintance, and to the succession of visitors (from America and Europe as well as Britain) who sought out the philosopher.

Mary too was increasingly conscious of the contradictions and tensions in her father's life and increasingly drawn to her real mother (whom she knew primarily through her father's writing and her own imagination). Her relationship with her step-mother was not good – and that with her step-sister Jane was tense. She relied on Fanny, as did Godwin, but neither wholly appreciated her.

Percy Shelley was not quite twenty (already expelled from Oxford and married with a child) when he wrote to Godwin in 1812 to introduce himself and register his surprise - and delight - that Godwin was still alive. For the best part of two years, in typically chaotic style, Shelley was forever about to arrive, and Godwin about to pounce on what looked like a financial saviour. They had finally settled matters to arrange a loan to solve Godwin's debts (on the basis of Shelley's inheritance prospects), when Mary returned from an extended stay in Scotland. As a radiant 16 year-old she entranced Shelley and was entranced by him. For Shelley, she was the daughter of the most radical and famous couple; for Mary, he represented a revivifying of the conviction and intellectual passion she had seen gradually extinguished in her father.

Godwin was outraged by their affair. He could not condone the relationship between the impressionable Mary and blithely irresponsible Shelley. There was too much feeling, too little reason. When they eloped, Godwin became a caricature of damaged pride, which he occasionally swallowed to cadge further financial assistance from Shelley. He coupled this with an almost vindictive withdrawal from his daughter, refusing to see her or to communicate with her. This hurt her deeply. So deeply that it is hard not to see her working out her distress and her conflicting emotions in her own writing – with Dr Frankenstein as the father figure who spurns his creation; and the creature wreaking destruction on Frankenstein's family to gain his attention and affection and to force Frankenstein to create a mate for him. The novel is a maelstrom of conflicting perspectives, emotions and demands – a cathartic expression of Mary's own sense of confusion, rejection, and dismay.

The reconciliation between Mary and her father comes with her marriage to Shelley, with which the play closes. It is not easy to like Godwin's letter to his brother two months after the wedding:

"The piece of news however I have to tell you is, that I went to church with this tall girl some time ago to be married. Her husband is the eldest son of Sir Thomas Shelley of Field Place in the county of Sussex, baronet. So that, according to the vulgar ideas of the world, she is well-married; and I have great hopes the young man will make her a good husband. You will wonder, I dare say, how a girl with not a penny of fortune, should meet with so good a match. But such are the ups and downs of this world. For my part I care comparatively little about wealth, so that it should be her destiny in life to be respectable, virtuous and contented."

The letter is a pompous and mangled but nonetheless genuine expression of Godwin's abiding pride in and love for his daughter. His love had a price: he was very demanding of her, for attention, help and support, and he expected a great deal of her – expectations which *Frankenstein* both vindicated and fuelled. These became still harder to meet in the years that followed, when two more of her children died, when Shelley drowned, and before her last child, Percy Florence Shelley, was formally accepted as the heir to the Shelley fortune, giving her some security. Yet for all his insensitivity and neediness, Godwin remained a central part of Mary's life, bound by the tragedies and experiences they had shared, and by their shared intellectual pursuits.

The story of Mary and her family is a complex one, replete with tragedy and heartbreak. Godwin's rationalism epitomised the optimism of the late enlightenment, but his actual life became increasingly gothic, dark, and subject to currents and forces he could not control. Mary's Frankenstein expresses her sense that when mind over-reaches it unleashes dangerous primitive emotions. In her early life, the expectation had been that reason and justice would order her world. But over and over again she encounters the reality as unruly and resistant - subject to powerful psychological forces that Godwin's rationalism left him ill-prepared to respond to, and to which she gives full rein in *Frankenstein*. In the end they held fast to each other among the wreckage but, as Mary Shelley eloquently attests, their lesson was learnt the hard way.

Dr Mark Philp is a Fellow and Tutor in Politics at Oriel College, University of Oxford.

A wide range of letters and papers from the family are available on-line at: www.bodley.ox.ac.uk/dept/scwmss/wmss/online/1500-1900/abinger/abinger.html

The journal kept by Shelley and Mary on their elopement to France, and sustained thereafter by Mary, has been published as: *The Journals of Mary Shelley*, 1814–1844, ed. by Paula R. Feldman and Diana Scott-Kilvert (Oxford and New York: Oxford University Press; Clarendon Press, 1987)

Godwin's detailed but cryptic diary is available on-line at: http://godwindiary.bodleian.ox.ac.uk Schools with A level students interested in undertaking projects in English or History associated with the Shelley–Godwin circle are encouraged to get in touch: godwindiary@politics.ox.ac.uk

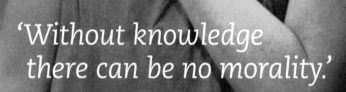

'Without knowledge
there can be no morality.'

Mary Wollstonecraft
A Vindication of The Rights of Woman

'There will be no war,
no crimes, no administration
of 'justice' and no government.
Every man will seek the good
of all…They will know they
are members of the chain
that each has his utility.'

William Godwin

The cast

Kristin Atherton
Mary Shelley

Kristin trained at the London Academy of Dramatic Art (LAMDA).

For Shared Experience: *Brontë* (Watermill, Oxford Playhouse and national tour); and *Mary Shelley* (West Yorkshire Playhouse Transform Festival and Bodleian Library).

Other theatre includes: *The Importance of Being Earnest* (English Theatre of Vienna); *Harold Pinter: A Celebration* (National Theatre); *Confessions of a City*, *Much Ado about Nothing*, *Iphigenia* (Sheffield Crucible); *A Tale of Two Dogs* (Out of Order, Dylan Thomas Centre); *Chimeras* (Liquid Theatre, Old Vic New Voices); *Lost Soul Music* (Pleasance Theatre) and *Bee Stings* (503 Theatre).

Radio and voiceover credits include: *I Love You S.W* (BBC Radio Drama); *The Fearless Youth* (Wireless Theatre, Roundhouse Radio); *Out and About* (Granada); and *Bible Geschichte* (Blautöne studios).

William Chubb
William Godwin

Theatre includes: Dr Kirby in *Eden End* (Northampton Theatre Royal and English Touring Theatre); Jeremy Burnham in *Yes, Prime Minister* (Gielgud Theatre); Holofernes in *Love's Labour's Lost* (Rose Theatre, Kingston); Richard Greatham in *Hay Fever* (Haymarket Theatre); Headmaster in *The History Boys* (National Theatre at Wyndham's); Finch McComus in *You Never Can Tell* (Garrick Theatre); Dr Emmerson in *Whose Life Is It Anyway* (Comedy Theatre); The Devil/Mendoza in *Man and Superman*, Ernest Friedman in *Design for Living* (Peter Hall Company at Theatre Royal Bath); Milton in *Homebody Kabul* (Cheek by Jowl at the Young Vic); Pastor Manders in *Ghosts* (English Touring Theatre); Karl Lindner in *A Raisin in the Sun* (Young Vic); Doja in *He Stumbled* and Holofernes in *Judith* (Wrestling School).

Television includes: *Law & Order*, *Silk*, *Trial and Retribution*, *Extremely Dangerous*, *The Ambassador*, *To Play the King*, *House of Cards*, *The Buddha of Suburbia*, *Sleepers*.

Ben Lamb
Percy Bysshe Shelley

Ben trained at RADA and graduated in 2010.

Theatre includes: *As You Like It* (Globe Theatre) and *Hamlet* (Sheffield Crucible).

Television includes: *Silk* (BBC).

Ben has also performed in *20 Cigarettes* (National Youth Theatre) and *The Dreaming* (National Youth Music Theatre).

Flora Nicholson
Fanny Godwin /
Mary Wollstonecraft
/ Harriet

Flora trained at Rose
Bruford College.

For Shared Experience: *Brontë*
(Watermill, Oxford Playhouse and
national tour) and *Mary Shelley* (West
Yorkshire Playhouse Transform
Festival and Bodleian Library).

Other theatre includes: *Bugs* (Factory
Theatre); *Blue Fence* (Pleasance Theatre);
Theatre Café (Company of Angels/
Unicorn Theatre); *The Great Irish Elk*
(Theatre 503), *Othello* (RSC); *Sons of
Bond* showcase at the Theatre Royal
Haymarket and the *Sam Wanamaker
Festival* (Shakespeare's Globe).
Rehearsed readings include: *Johnson
Lives* directed by Tim Piggott-Smith
(Hampstead Theatre); *Antigone* and
Ensnared (Soho Theatre).

Television includes: *The Thai Bride,
Doctors* and the *Royal Today.*

Film includes: *Winter Sun* (short).

Sadie Shimmin
Mrs Godwin

Theatre includes:
*Vanity Fair, Pericles,
Andromache* (Cheek
by Jowl); *Wild Oats,
Life After Life, The Rose Tattoo,* (National
Theatre and UK tour); *'Night Mother*
(The Old Red Lion); *You Can't Take
It With You* (Southwark Playhouse);
A Voyage Round My Father (Donmar
Warehouse and Wyndhams);
The Crucible (Sheffield Crucible);
Mensch Meier (Leicester Haymarket);
*A Midsummer Night's Dream,
The Importance of Being Earnest* (Oldham
Coliseum); *Lucy's Play* (Traverse);

Schippel the Plumber (Greenwich and
Lyceum, Edinburgh); *Control Freaks*
(BAC); and *The Tin Horizon, Cold Hands*
(Theatre 503). Sadie also regularly
performs with Shorts at the Landor,
a new writing event, at The Landor
Theatre, London.

Television includes: *Silk, Whitechapel,
Holby City, The Nativity, Upstairs
Downstairs* and *Coronation Street.*
Sadie also played Chief of Police
Lisa Holgersson in series 1 and 2
of *Wallander* for the BBC and the
Young Crone in *Blackadder 2.*

Radio credits include: Two series of
All The Young Dudes and *A Voyage
Round My Father* (BBC Radio 4).

Shannon Tarbet
Jane Clairmont / Maid

Theatre includes:
Skåne (Hampstead
Theatre); *66 Books*
(Bush Theatre);
The Flooded Grave (Bush Theatre/
Latitude Festival); *Mogadishu*
(Manchester Royal Exchange and
Lyric Hammersmith) for which
Shannon was nominated as Best
Actress in a Supporting Role in the
Manchester Theatre Awards; and *Spur
of the Moment* (Royal Court) shortlisted
for the Evening Standard Theatre
Award for Outstanding Newcomer.

Television includes: *Lewis* (ITV),
Monroe (ITV); *Silk* and *Inspector
George Gently* (BBC).

Film includes: *Woodlands, Lost
and Found* and *Just Cracked* (short).

Radio includes: *Skyvers, Mogadishu,
All the Blood in My Veins* (BBC Radio).

The creative team

Helen Edmundson
Writer

Helen Edmundson's relationship with Shared Experience is a long and fruitful one, including five previous stage adaptations for the company: *Anna Karenina* and *The Mill on the Floss* – both of which toured nationally and internationally; *War and Peace*, which was produced at the National Theatre in 1996 and again on tour in 2008; *Gone to Earth*, which was seen on tour and at the Lyric Hammersmith in 2003 and *Orestes*, at The Tricycle and on tour in 2006.

Other work in theatre has included:
The Clearing, first performed at the Bush Theatre; *Mother Teresa is Dead* at the The Royal Court Theatre; *The Heresy of Love*, produced by the RSC at the Swan Theatre in Winter 2012; an adaptation of *Coram Boy*, which premiered at the National Theatre in 2005 and was revived the following year and on Broadway; a new version of Calderon's *Life is a Dream* at The Donmar in 2009, and a musical version of *Swallows and Amazons*, (co-written with Neil Hannen), which premiered at Bristol Old Vic in 2010 before transferring to the Vaudeville Theatre in 2011 and embarking on a nationwide tour in 2012.

The Clearing received the John Whiting Award for best new play, as well as a Time Out Award. She also won TMA and Time Out Awards for *The Mill on the Floss*, *Anna Karenina* and a Time Out Award for *Coram Boy*.

Helen has written two short films for television: *One Day* for BBC2 and *Stella* for Channel 4. She has undertaken a number of adaptations for BBC Radio, including Virginia Woolf's *The Voyage Out*, Hardy's *The Mayor of Casterbridge*, and Arnold Bennett's *Anna of the Five Towns*.

She is currently under commission with the National Theatre, and with Roundabout, New York, for whom she is writing an adaptation of *Thérèse Raquin* to be produced later this year.

Polly Teale
Director

Polly Teale has created a unique body of work as a writer and director that has won critical and audience acclaim with productions transferring to the West End and touring internationally. An award-winning theatre practitioner, she has been joint artistic director of Shared Experience since 1995. She has also authored a number of original plays and stage adaptations, including *Jane Eyre* and *Brontë*, and *After Mrs Rochester* for which she won the Evening Standard Award for Best Director and the Time Out Award for Best West End Production.

Other recent directing credits include:
Speechless (co-writer/director), *The Glass Menagerie*, *Mine* (writer/director), *Ten Tiny Toes*, *Kindertransport*, *Madame Bovary*, *The Clearing*, *A Doll's House*, *The House of Bernarda Alba*, *Desire Under the Elms*, and, as co-director, *War and Peace* (co-production with National Theatre) and *Mill on the Floss*.

Polly has also written a screenplay of her 2003 play, *Brontë*, which has recently been sold to Pathé who plan to make it into a feature film.

Naomi Dawson
Designer

Naomi is a freelance theatre designer. She trained at Wimbledon School of Art and Kunstacademie, Maastricht. Since graduating she has worked predominantly in theatre, with a particular interest in new writing, both in the UK and abroad.

Work with Shared Experience includes: *The Glass Menagerie* (Salisbury Playhouse and Tour); and *Speechless* (Traverse, Sherman Cymru, national tour).

Other recent theatre design work includes: *Belongings* (Hampstead/Trafalgar Studio); *Love and Money* (Stadsteater, Malmo); a version of Kafka's *Amerika* (Staatstheater, Mainz); *The Gods Weep* (RSC, Hampstead Theatre); *In Praise of Love* (Theatre Royal, Northampton); *The Typist* (Broadcast live on Sky Arts); *Krieg Der Bilder* (Staatstheater, Mainz); *Rutherford and Son* (Northern Stage); *Three More Sleepless Nights* (Lyttelton, National Theatre); *The Container* (Young Vic); *King Pelican*; *Speed Death of the Radiant Child* (Drum Theatre, Plymouth); *Amgen: Broken* (Sherman Cymru); *If That's All There Is* (Lyric), *State of Emergency* (Gate); *...Sisters* (Gate/Headlong); and *Phaedra's Love* (Barbican Pit and Bristol Old Vic).

Naomi is part of artists collective, SpRoUt, recently exhibiting in Galerija SC, Zagreb, creating an installation for the exhibition Under Construction –

Staging the Future which explores the nature of collaboration, staged-spaces and links between the past and the future.

Keith Clouston
Composer

Theatre credits include: *A Midsummer Night's Dream, King Lear, The Winter's Tale, Julius Caesar, Coriolanus, Night of the Soul* (RSC); *The UN Inspector* (National Theatre); *The Resistible Rise of Arturo Ui, The Magic Carpet* (Lyric Hammersmith); *Baghdad Wedding* (Soho); *The Eleventh Capita!* (Royal Court); *Tamburlaine* (Bristol Old Vic/Barbican); *A Midsummer Night's Dream, Comedy of Errors, Paradise Lost, Twelfth Night, Cyrano de Bergerac* (Bristol Old Vic); *Electra, Trojan Women* (Cambridge Greek Play, Cambridge Arts).

Credits as a musical director include: *Mojo* (Barbican) and as assistant sound designer *Speechless* (Shared Experience/Sherman Cymru).

Credits as a musician include: Within theatre: *The Comedy of Errors* (Shakespeare's Globe); and *Peer Gynt* (National Theatre). Within television: *Later with Jools Holland, The Girlie Show, Painted Lady, The Life of Mohammed, Glastonbury '99* and *The Bill*. Within film: *Beloved* (musician); and *Private Peaceful* (arranger/musician).

Radio credits include: *Wedding* (BBC Radio 3); *The Andy Kershaw Show* (BBC Radio 1), *Loose Ends* (BBC Radio 4), *Antony and Cleopatra* and *The Iliad* (BBC Radio 3).

Liz Ranken
Movement Director

Liz has a long-standing relationship with Shared Experience, having worked on many of the company's productions. She is a founder member of DV8, Associate Movement Director at the RSC and has worked extensively with Dominic Cooke. She is the winner of the 1992 Dance Umbrella Time Out Award, The Place Portfolio Choreographic Award (Artists to Invest In) and a Capital Award at the Edinburgh Fringe Festival.

Chris Davey
Lighting Designer

For Shared Experience: *Speechless, The Caucasian Chalk Circle, Jane Eyre, Brontë, Madame Bovary, After Mrs Rochester, A Passage to India, The Mill on the Floss, Anna Karenina, The Tempest, Desire Under the Elms, The Danube, War and Peace.*

Chris has designed extensively for West Yorkshire Playhouse, National Theatre, RSC, Royal Court, Hampstead Theatre, Lyric Hammersmith, Royal Exchange Manchester, Royal Lyceum Edinburgh, Birmingham Rep, Opera North, Welsh National Opera and Dutch National Opera.

Other recent designs include: *Lord of the Flies* (New Adventures); *She Loves Me* (Chichester); *King Lear* and *Waiting for Godot* (West Yorkshire Playhouse); *Beasts and Beauties* (Hampstead); *As You Like It* (Royal Exchange Manchester); *Shoes* (Sadler's Wells); *Carlos Acosta: Premieres Plus* (London Coliseum); *The Pianist, Everyone Loves a Winner, Carlos Acosta* (Manchester International Festival / Sadler's Wells); *The Last Witch* (Edinburgh International Festival / Traverse) and *Peer Gynt* (National Theatre of Scotland).

Chris has won the TMA Best Lighting Design for *Dial M for Murder* (West Yorkshire Playhouse) and *Beyond the Horizon* (Royal and Derngate, Northampton).

Drew Baumohl
Sound Designer

Drew trained at Bristol Old Vic Theatre School and is currently employed as Deputy Head of Lighting and Sound at Nottingham Playhouse.

Drew's previous sound designs include: *Umbrellas, Private Lives, Amy's View, Twelfth Night, The Families of Lockerbie, A Day in the Death of Joe Egg, Forever Young, Blithe Spirit, Glamour, Vertigo, Tom's Midnight Garden, Beast on the Moon* and *Aladdin* (Nottingham Playhouse Theatre Company); *The Crossing* (New Art Exchange); *The Trial, Blood Wedding, The Visit, Find Me* and *Down in the Dumps* (Nottingham Playhouse Youth Theatre); *West Side Story* (Nottingham Operatic Society); *Séance on a Sunday Afternoon, Empty Bed Blues* and *Smile* (Lakeside Arts Centre); *Thoroughly Modern Millie, Crazy For You* (Carlton Operatic Society); and as Associate Sound Designer, *Summer and Smoke* (Apollo Theatre, London).

Lauren Harvey
Deputy Stage Manager

Lauren graduated from the University of Birmingham with a BA Honours in Drama and Theatre Arts in 2008, and then went on to complete a Post Graduate Diploma in Technical Theatre (specialising in Stage Management) at Mountview Academy of Theatre Arts.

Previous professional experience as a Deputy Stage Manager include: *Piano/Forte*, *The President of an Empty Room* and *The Storm* (Birmingham School of Acting).

As an Assistant Stage Manager:
Speechless (Shared Experience); *Love Love Love* (Paines Plough UK Tour); *I'm a Playwright get me out of Here*, *Tales of the Harrow Road*, *Behud and Shradda* (Soho Theatre).

As a Company Manager: *Dr. Faustus* (Stratford Circus).

Cecily Boys
Assistant Director

Cecily trained at York University.

Credits as a Director include: *Talking in Bed* (Theatre 503); *Edem* (Jermyn Street Theatre); *Bed, Pinter...esque, Hang Up, Waiting for Godot, Oleanna* (Old Bomb Theatre at York Theatre Royal); *Pitch Perfect* (Tristan Bates Theatre); *Office Song* (White Bear Theatre); *The Merchant of Venice, As You Like It* (York Shakespeare Company); *Dogg's Hamlet & Cahoot's Macbeth* (Play On Theatre) and *Journey's End* (Stagecoach Youth Theatre York).

Credits as an Associate Director include: *Antigone* (Southwark Playhouse) and *Fair Trade* (Shatterbox Theatre Company).

Credits as an Assistant Director include: *Three Days in May* (Trafalgar Studios and tour), *Lysistrata* (Rose Theatre, Kingston), *All I Want For Christmas* (Jermyn Street Theatre) *This Story Of Yours* (Old Red Lion), *Decade* (Theatre 503), *Madagascar* (Primavera Productions), *Twelfth Night, The White Crow* (York Theatre Royal). Cecily is Artistic Director of Old Bomb Theatre Company.

SHARED
EXPERIENCE

Your support now will make the difference

- **30 years of changing the landscape of British theatre**

- **★★★★★ productions**

- **Seen by thousands of people across the UK and abroad**

- **Led by two of the UK's foremost directors**

- **Nurturing new writers, actors and theatremakers**

- **Inspiring audiences of all ages**

Shared Experience is under threat, following the cut of its core funding by Arts Council England. The theatre company is determined to find a way to survive and to continue to make trailblazing theatre. To do that, it needs your help. ACE has said that it wants the company to continue but can only support it with project funding, which helps to fund individual productions. This leaves a hole of around £83,000 per annum needed to cover core salaries, fund the delivery of educational activity in schools, provide a rehearsal space and commission new plays for future productions.

Without you there is no Shared Experience

To find out how you can make a difference email
supportus@sharedexperience.org.uk

Anne Marie Duff in A Doll's House

Shared Experience

30 Years of ground-breaking theatre

Education

Shared Experience is a recommended practitioner on the AQA syllabus. The education team offers workshops and theatre events to support all Shared Experience productions, through which students are able to gain a deeper understanding of the company's unique rehearsal process. Two-hour workshops are available for Drama and English Literature students for ages 14+ and can be tailored for groups studying at GCSE, A-Level or Higher Education levels.

A *Mary Shelley* Resource Pack is available to download FREE from our website at **www.sharedexperience.org.uk**

For Shared Experience

Artistic Director	Polly Teale
Artistic Director	Nancy Meckler
Producer	Michelle Knight
Producer's Assistant	Hannah Bevan
Marketing	Erin Crivelli, Russell Souch, Lisa Wood
Press	Madeleine Woolgar
London Marketing	Mark Slaughter
London Press	Clíona Roberts
Production Photography	Robert Day

Board of Directors
Chair: Joan Bakewell
Diane Benjamin
Geoff Westmore
Neil Brener
George Carey
Olga Edridge
Clare Lawrence Moody
Alistair Petrie
Alan Rivett
Mary Roscoe

Patrons
Sarah and Neil Brener
Paula Clemett and
Geoff Westmore
Lady Hatch
Ann Orton

Shared Experience
Oxford Playhouse, Beaumont Street, Oxford OX1 2LW
T:01865 305301 **sharedexperience.org.uk**

 /sharedexperience **@setheatre**

Brontë, photo: Robert Day

WY PLAY HOUSE

Co-Producer of *Mary Shelley*

Since opening in 1990, West Yorkshire Playhouse has established a national and international reputation, providing both a thriving focal point for the communities of West Yorkshire and theatre of the highest standard for audiences throughout the region and beyond.

We are delighted to be working once again with Shared Experience, a regular partner of the Playhouse, and Nottingham Playhouse to create this world premiere production of **Mary Shelley** which enjoyed development time as part of West Yorkshire Playhouse's **Transform** 2011 Festival. Our last collaboration was a new translation of Brecht's **The Caucasian Chalk Circle** by Alistair Beaton in 2009.

West Yorkshire Playhouse welcomed over 60,000 people for our Christmas season with a critically acclaimed new production of **Annie** and our reinvented **Jack and the Beanstalk**. **Waiting for Godot**, a co-production with Talawa Theatre Company, tours nationally and we recently staged the world premiere of **Angus, Thongs and Even More Snogging**, based on the books by Louise Rennison. To complete the season, a new production

Caucasian Chalk Circle 2009

of Tom Stoppard's classic comedy **The Real Thing**, co-produced with English Touring Theatre will play the Quarry Theatre prior to a national tour; **Transform** 2012 Festival in April will welcome twelve companies and fifteen individual artists into the Playhouse to develop new ways of working and create theatre over two intense celebratory weekends and the New Writing Season will extol and explore the state of new writing in theatre today. The season ends with another world premiere, the new high-energy musical **Loserville**, by Elliot Davis and James Bourne.

To produce the most exciting work and give longer-life to our productions, West Yorkshire Playhouse regularly joins forces with producing theatres and companies to create new productions. Most recently we worked with Northampton Theatre Royal, Derby Live and Perfect Pitch to launch the world premiere of the musical of *The Go-Between*. We have coproduced many large scale musical works as well as classic plays with Birmingham Repertory Theatre Company. Other partners include fellow producing theatres Liverpool Everyman and Playhouse, Lyric Theatre, Hammersmith, Bristol Old Vic, Hampstead Theatre, Polka Theatre and Theatre Royal Bath Productions as well as the most distinctive theatre companies working in the UK today Kneehigh Theatre, Told by an Idiot, Peepolykus, Improbable, English Touring Theatre, Talawa Theatre Company, Eclipse Theatre and Northern Broadsides and partners from the commercial sector Fiery Angel, All Banged Up, David Pugh, CMP and Sonia Friedman Productions.

King Lear 2011

And many of our productions transfer to London's West End including: *Ying Tong* (2004) to the New Ambassadors Theatre, *The Postman Always Rings Twice* (2005) to the Playhouse Theatre, Peepolykus' *The Hound Of The Baskervilles* (2007) to the Duchess Theatre; Kneehigh Theatre's *Brief Encounter* (2007) created with Birmingham Repertory Theatre Company, to the Cinema, Haymarket and Northern Broadsides' *Othello*, featuring Lenny Henry, to the Trafalgar Studios. The Tony and Olivier award-winning *The 39 Steps*, which was co-produced by West Yorkshire Playhouse with Fiery Angel in 2005, has played for 5 years at the Criterion Theatre in London and the run continues.

Artistic Director	Ian Brown
Chief Executive	Sheena Wrigley
Producer	Henrietta Duckworth
Director of Fundraising & Development	David Israel
Director of Communications	Su Matthewman
Finance Director	Helen Nakhwal
Director of Arts Development	Sam Perkins

wyp.org.uk

0113 213 7700

 /westyorkshireplayhouse

 @WYPlayhouse

Waiting for Godot

6 - 10 March
The Albany
thealbany.org.uk

13 - 17 March
The Old Rep
birmingham-rep.co.uk

27 - 31 March
Winchester Theatre Royal
theatre-royal-winchester.co.uk

3 - 7 April
New Wolsey Theatre
wolseytheatre.co.uk

The Real Thing

29 May - 2 June
Cambridge Arts Theatre
cambridgeartstheatre.com
01223 503 333

5 - 9 June
The Everyman Theatre,
Cheltenham
everymantheatre.org.uk
01242 572 573

12 - 16 June
Watford Palace Theatre
watfordpalacetheatre.co.uk
01923 235455

19 - 23 June
Theatre Royal Brighton
0844 871 7627

26 - 30 June
Oxford Playhouse
oxfordplayhouse.com
01865 305305

3 - 7 July
Northcott Theatre
exeternorthcott.co.uk
01392 493 493

Waiting for Godot 2012

Nottingham Playhouse

Co-Producer of *Mary Shelley*

Nottingham Playhouse is guided by its mission to make bold and thrilling theatre that is world-class.

We are delighted to be collaborating with Shared Experience and West Yorkshire Playhouse, in association with Oxford Playhouse, to produce *Mary Shelley*. This partnership is the latest in a rich history of successful collaborations with other UK theatres to bring the best new work to Nottingham and beyond.

Our belief in the power of collaboration has resulted in some outstanding theatre. Our recent co-productions with Liverpool Everyman and Playhouse Theatres include a new production of Bertolt Brecht's *The Resistible Rise of Arturo Ui*, directed by the Young Vic's Associate Director, Walter Meierjohann and a new adaptation of Sophocles' *Oedipus* by Steven Berkoff. Both plays received rapturous reviews, locally and nationally. Our spring season includes partnerships with Headlong and The Nuffield, Southampton, in association with Hull Truck Theatre to bring a new production of *Romeo & Juliet* and Mercury Theatre Colchester to bring audiences *Roots* in Arnold Wesker's 80th year.

In December 2013, Nottingham Playhouse celebrates 50 years in its existing building. During those 50 years the Playhouse stage has played host to many outstanding performers and helped create a generation of dedicated theatre-goers in the East Midlands. The work of Nottingham Playhouse is always evolving and in 2011 the organisation lead on a new festival – NEAT 11 – which saw venues across Nottingham celebrate the very best European theatre, dance, music, performance, film and visual art for adults and children. The festival is scheduled to return in 2014.

To find out more about our work please call **0115 947 4361** or visit **nottinghamplayhouse.co.uk**

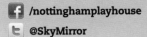 **/nottinghamplayhouse**

@SkyMirror

Artistic Director Giles Croft
Chief Executive Stephanie Sirr

 Supported by
ARTS COUNCIL ENGLAND

Nottingham Playhouse is a registered charity No. 1109342

Play your part in making great theatre

Every penny counts

Nottingham Playhouse is a registered charity (number 1109342) and the support of individual donors and local businesses is vital to help us continue to create world-class theatre here in Nottingham, and to deliver even more groundbreaking education and community projects locally.

We cannot do what we do without gifts from patrons and audience members.

Please do consider making a donation of any size when you book – either with our friendly Box Office team or online – it really is so important to the future of live theatre in Nottingham.

We are currently fundraising to support a revival of our trailblazing piece of theatre for young people with profound and multiple learning disabilities – White Peacock

See more for less with a Backstage Pass

One very simple way that you can help us to ensure the future of world class theatre in Nottingham is by joining our membership scheme **Backstage Pass**. It's your opportunity to support our work while also enjoying a fantastic range of benefits:

- Two FREE preview tickets
- Up to 50% off every Nottingham Playhouse Theatre Company show
- Up to 50% off selected visiting drama, music and dance
- Two free Nottingham Playhouse programmes
- Freedom from postage and booking fees
- 20% off drinks and à la carte dining for up to 4 in CAST
- Extra discounts at other local restaurants, shops and venues
- Exclusive newsletters, email updates and invitations to special events

A year's membership costs **£30** a year with ticket discounts for two people or **£40** for up to six: such a bargain that it could easily pay for itself within a couple of visits. And if you're under 26, or a member of Club Encore, membership is half price.

To find out more, call **0115 941 9419** or visit **nottinghamplayhouse.co.uk.**

The University of
Nottingham

UNITED KINGDOM · CHINA · MALAYSIA

Learn.
Try.
Explore...

The University's Open Day for the community
A free, fun and interactive day for all ages and interests

Saturday 19 May 2012

11am-5.30pm
University Park, NG7 2QL
t: +44 (0) 115 846 7155
e: mayfest@nottingham.ac.uk
www.nottingham.ac.uk/mayfest
#mayfest

WY PLAY HOUSE

Fri 16 March to Sat 7 April
Box Office: 0113 213 7700
wyp.org.uk

Nottingham Playhouse

Tue 17 April to Sat 5 May
Box Office: 0115 941 9419
nottinghamplayhouse.co.uk

National tour

Wed 9 to Sat 12 May
Box Office: 0151 709 4776
everymanplayhouse.com

Tue 29 May to Sat 2 June
Ticket Office: 01865 305 305
oxfordplayhouse.com

Tue 15 to Sat 19 May
Box Office: 01482 323 638
hulltruck.co.uk

Wed 6 to Sat 9 June
Box Office: 01962 840 440
theatre-royal-winchester.co.uk

Tue 22 to Sat 26 May
Box Office: 0191 230 5151
northernstage.co.uk

Tue 12 June to Sat 7 July
Box Office: 020 7328 1000
tricycle.co.uk

Special thanks to

Mark Bentley
Maxwell Hutcheon
Clare Lawrence-Moody
Dr Mark Philp
Alex Robertson
Peter Salem
Maya Wasowicz
University of Oxford's Bodleian Library

Helen Edmundson

MARY SHELLEY

NICK HERN BOOKS
www.nickhernbooks.co.uk

SHARED EXPERIENCE
www.sharedexperience.org.uk

Mary Shelley was first performed in a co-production between Shared Experience, Nottingham Playhouse and West Yorkshire Playhouse, at the West Yorkshire Playhouse, Leeds, on 16 March 2012, with the following cast:

MARY	Kristin Atherton
FANNY	Flora Nicholson
MRS GODWIN	Sadie Shimmin
JANE	Shannon Tarbet
WILLIAM GODWIN	William Chubb
PERCY SHELLEY	Ben Lamb

Director	Polly Teale
Designer	Naomi Dawson
Composer	Keith Coulston
Lighting Designer	Chris Davey
Sound Designer	Drew Baumohl
Movement Director	Liz Ranken

The production subsequently toured to Nottingham Playhouse; Liverpool Playhouse; Hull Truck Theatre; Northern Stage, Newcastle; Oxford Playhouse; Winchester Theatre Royal and the Tricycle Theatre, London.

Mary Shelley: A Timeline

1792
Mary Wollstonecraft's feminist *A Vindication of the Rights of Woman* is published.

1793
William Godwin's radical political treatise, *Enquiry Concerning Political Justice,* is published.

1797
Mary Wollstonecraft marries William Godwin in St Pancras Church, London. Wollstonecraft already has one daughter, Fanny (b. May 1794), by Gilbert Imlay.

August
Mary Wollstonecraft gives birth to Mary Wollstonecraft Godwin.

September
Mary Wollstonecraft dies – her daughter, Mary, is only eleven days old.

1801
William Godwin marries Mary Jane Vial. Mary Jane already has a daughter, Jane Clairmont (b. 1798) aged twenty-one.

1814
Mary Godwin meets Percy Bysshe Shelley and they embark on a relationship. Percy is twenty-two years old and married. His wife, Harriet, is pregnant with their second child.

July
William Godwin disapproves of the relationship. Percy leaves his wife and family and flees to Europe with Mary, just sixteen, and her stepsister, Jane.

November
Percy's estranged wife, Harriet Shelley, gives birth to their second child, Charles.

1815
February
Mary gives birth to her first child with Percy – Clara. Clara dies at just thirteen days old.

1816
January
Mary gives birth to a son, William.

May
Percy, Mary and their son William leave for a tour of Europe. Mary's stepsister Jane also joins them (pregnant with Lord Byron's child). The weather takes a turn for the worse and they are confined indoors. Byron challenges the group to write their own ghost stories. It is here that Mary begins to write her acclaimed novel *Frankenstein*.

October
Mary's half-sister, Fanny Imlay, commits suicide in Swansea, aged twenty-two.

December
After being missing for a month, Percy's wife, Harriet Shelley, is found in the Serpentine River, Hyde Park, London. She was twenty-one years old and heavily pregnant at the time of her death.

A pregnant Mary marries Percy at St Mildred's Church in London. She is reconciled with her father.

1818

Frankenstein: or, The Modern Prometheus is anonymously published in three volumes and to immediate success.

May
Mary writes her mythological drama, *Proserpine*, written for children. Percy contributes two poems to the piece.

September
Mary's daughter Clara dies from dysentery in Venice.

1819

Mary and Percy's three-year-old son William dies of cholera in Italy.

November
Mary gives birth to their fourth child, Percy Florence.

1822

Percy Bysshe Shelley drowns when his boat capsizes in the Gulf of Spezia. He is cremated and buried in Rome.

1824

Following her return to England with her son, Mary tries to publish a selection of Percy's poems but Percy's father, Sir Timothy Shelley, demands that she cease all writing and publications about his late son.

April
Lord Byron dies in Greece.

1826

Mary Shelley's *The Last Man* is published – an apocalyptic novel that tells of a future world that has been ravaged by a plague.

1832

Mary's half-brother, William, dies (son of William Godwin and Mary Jane Vial).

1836

Mary's father, William Godwin dies.

1837

Mary's last novel, *Falkner*, which charts a young woman's education under a tyrannical father figure, is published.

1839

A collection of Percy Bysshe Shelley's poems are finally published with Sir Timothy Shelley's permission.

1844

Sir Timothy Shelley dies. Mary's son, Percy Florence, inherits the estate and title.

1848

Percy Florence Shelley marries Jane Gibson.

1851

Mary Shelley dies from a brain tumour after a long illness.

To Shared Experience

Characters

MARY
MARY WOLLSTONECRAFT, *as imagined by Mary*
FANNY
MRS GODWIN
JANE
WILLIAM GODWIN
PERCY SHELLEY
HARRIET
MAID
And a SAILOR, CROWDS OF PEOPLE

Heartfelt thanks to Dr Mark Philp for his tireless help and advice.

H.E.

This text went to press before the end of rehearsals and so may differ slightly from the play as performed.

ACT ONE

Scene One

*March 1814. The mouth of the Thames. MARY is standing
alone on the deck of a ship. There is a book in her hands.*

MARY (*reading*). 'Her first thought had led her to Battersea
Bridge, but she found it too public. It was night when she
arrived at Putney, and by that time it had begun to rain with
great violence. The rain suggested to her the idea of walking
up and down the bridge until her clothes were thoroughly
drenched and heavy with the wet.'

We are plunged into MARY*'s imagination. Darkness. Rain
lashes down.*

We see a woman – MARY WOLLSTONECRAFT *– holding
out her arms to the elements, drenching herself. Then she
climbs onto the edge of the bridge and jumps into the water.
We hear the sound of the water pounding in her ears, see her
struggle to stay under, groaning and wailing with frustration.
Finally she becomes senseless, giving herself to the water.*

Mother…

Scene Two

*A wharf. London docks. MARY has disembarked and stands on
the quay. It is noisy and crowded. People hurry past her. A
SAILOR puts her trunk down next to her. She gives him a penny
and he leaves.*

FANNY *approaches her through the crowd.*

FANNY. Mary! Mary!

MARY. Fanny!

FANNY *rushes to her. They embrace*.

FANNY. Oh, Mary. You're home. You're home at last.

MARY. Are you alone? Father wrote that he would come.

FANNY. He wanted to, indeed he did. But he got called to a meeting with some lawyers and…

MARY. Lawyers?

FANNY. Don't worry. But how cold you are. Why didn't you stay below?

MARY. Oh, you know I can't bear to be below. It makes me feel sicker than ever. And besides, I was reading this – (*Holds out the book*.) and I wanted to read it with water churning beneath me and a wild wind banging in my ears.

FANNY. What is it?

MARY. Fanny… it's Father's memoir of our mother. And I cannot tell you what a revelation it has been.

FANNY. Mary…

MARY. I've read it over and over. I feel as if I know her and love her a hundred times better than I did before. I feel as if she could be standing here right now, and I would slip my arm through hers and kiss her cheek quite naturally, for she is real to me.

FANNY. Where did you get this?

MARY. Did you know that our mother tried to kill herself? It was after your father left her. She was so desperate, broken. She threw herself into the river. This river.

FANNY. Hush.

It's against the law, Mary.

MARY. Did you know? Did you?

FANNY. I thought something like that had happened. Yes.

MARY. When I first read it, I was sitting alone on a beach in Scotland, with the waves coming towards me and coming towards me. I almost knew what was going to happen before

I saw the words. They're Father's words, so they are quite measured and restrained, but I could imagine it all beneath the lines – her agony, her desire to have it all stop. I almost wished the waters had taken her, for that is what she truly wanted, but then, if they had, I would not be here upon this earth – whatever this earth might be.

FANNY. Where did you get this from?

MARY. It was on Father's shelves. He said I could take whatever I liked before I left.

FANNY. But he didn't mean this.

MARY. Why not? It's a published work. Hundreds of people have read it. He wouldn't want to hide the truth from us. Truth is omnipotent.

FANNY. Truth. I sometimes think our family speaks a great deal too much truth. I wish we could be like normal people, and keep our thoughts to ourselves.

MARY. But that would be cowardly.

Are we not normal people then?

FANNY. You know we aren't.

MARY. Oh, don't be cross, Fanny. This is a precious discovery. I mean to read it to you.

FANNY. No.

MARY. Yes. We'll read a little every night. Our mother would have wanted that. I know she would.

FANNY (*gazing at the book*). 'Your real mother was only too ready to leave you behind.'

That's what Mama said. 'Your real mother didn't even think of you when she tried to end it all.'

MARY. She said that? When? How dare she say that to you?

FANNY. It doesn't matter. I didn't tell you so you would be cross with Mama.

MARY. Don't call her Mama. She's not our mama. She's just the dreadful creature who my father has the misfortune to be married to.

FANNY. Mary…

MARY. Your real mother did think about you. She must have felt that you would be better off being raised by others. She was so wretched.

FANNY. Perhaps.

MARY. Our poor mother. You could not cheer her with all your sweetness, and I… I was the cause of her death.

FANNY. Please don't make trouble with Mama – I mean, with Mrs Godwin – when we get home. You won't, will you?

MARY. No. I won't. I have come home determined to rise above the dreadful Mrs Godwin. I intend to remain completely aloof.

How are things at Skinner Street? How is dear Papa?

FANNY. He is very much occupied, but in reasonably good spirits.

MARY. And have you been lonely, with everyone away?

FANNY. I haven't had time. Mama has started another translation, so there's been a great deal of copying to do. And I've been writing letters for Papa and running errands and minding the shop. Jane arrived home from school two days ago. She was going to come with me to meet you, but then she discovered I was walking here and…

MARY. That's so like her.

FANNY. We shall get a chaise back, of course. Papa put some money by.

And we have some new friends.

MARY. Do we?

FANNY. Do you remember a young man – one of Papa's disciples – who wrote him all those elaborate letters that he used to read out to us?

MARY. Do you mean the man called Shelley?

FANNY. Yes. Well, he's in London now. He talks and talks philosophy with Papa. He says *Political Justice* is his bible.

MARY. Isn't he a baronet or something of the sort?

FANNY. He's the heir to a baronetcy. His grandfather is Sir Bysshe Shelley of Sussex.

MARY. How grand.

FANNY. He wants to help us. He wants to invest in the bookshop.

MARY. Really?

FANNY. And he is quite… extraordinary.

MARY. In what way?

FANNY. He's… I don't know how to explain it… He's so vibrant. More vibrant than anyone I ever met. And he speaks to me so easily. I feel I could talk to him about anything.

MARY. Fanny Godwin… I do believe you are in love.

FANNY. I'm not. I'm not. He's married.

MARY. But that doesn't stop you from falling in love.

FANNY. His wife is… quite lovely. Quite a fine lady. But you shall see all this. Come now, my poor cold girl. Let's find a chaise and get you home.

Scene Three

The parlour. Skinner Street. A window looks out onto the street, and from outside the noise of a crowd can be heard.

MARY *and* FANNY *set the trunk down.* MRS GODWIN *enters.*

MRS GODWIN. Move that trunk out of the way, Mary. What makes you think we want that in the middle of the parlour?

MARY. I'm a little tired. I'll move it soon.

MRS GODWIN. You went away for your health, you shouldn't have come back tired.

MARY. I'm tired from the journey, that's all.

MRS GODWIN. Well, we're all tired. Now move it.

FANNY. I'll move it.

MARY. No, leave it, Fanny. I'll do it.

MRS GODWIN. Go and help Jane with the tea things, Fanny.

FANNY. Yes, Mama.

> FANNY *leaves*. MRS GODWIN *begins to set up a small table for tea*. MARY *moves the trunk*.

MARY. Can't the maid see to the tea?

MRS GODWIN. The maid doesn't work today. She does three days now. We had less need of her with everyone away. Everyone has to do their bit, that's all.

> (*Calling*.) Mr Godwin! Tea!

> Charles is doing awfully well in Edinburgh.

MARY. Yes. He wrote to me.

MRS GODWIN. But you didn't see him, I suppose?

MARY. No.

MRS GODWIN. I would have thought you might want to visit your stepbrother, with him being so close.

MARY. It's quite some distance from Dundee to Edinburgh. We made do with letters.

MRS GODWIN. I don't know why he had to go so far away. There are plenty of apprenticeships to be had in London. Why go all the way to Scotland?

MARY. I can't imagine.

MRS GODWIN (*calling*). Mr Godwin! If you don't come out, we shall come in!

> Every day.

MARY. There's really no need to disturb his work. I can see him at dinner.

JANE *enters*. MARY *goes to the window and looks out*.

JANE. Maman, Fanny wants to know if we should put all the sugar buns out?

MRS GODWIN. All of them? Of course not. One each. We're not elephants.

JANE *goes to the window*.

JANE. Gracious, what a crowd. I wonder who they're hanging?

MRS GODWIN (*to* MARY). And you left the Baxters tolerably well, I hope?

MARY. I'm sorry…?

MRS GODWIN. The Baxters. You left them tolerably well?

MARY. Yes. They were fine, thank you.

MRS GODWIN. Did they send their regards to me?

MARY. To my father and to you, yes.

MRS GODWIN. Oh. Then you should pass them on. Not leave me to prise them out of you.

(*Calling*.) Mr Godwin!

She leaves. JANE *and* MARY *listen to the crowd passing by*.

JANE. Isn't hanging the most awful thing? So primitive, don't you think, Mary? So utterly barbaric.

GODWIN *enters from the study*.

GODWIN. What is utterly barbaric?

MARY. Hanging.

GODWIN. Ah, yes. That would qualify.

MARY. Hello, Papa.

MARY *goes to him and kisses his cheek with great affection*.

GODWIN. Well, well. Hello to you too.

MRS GODWIN *enters, holding a tablecloth*.

MRS GODWIN. Finally, he emerges.

GODWIN. I'm sorry, Mrs Godwin, am I horribly late? Have I missed tea?

MRS GODWIN. No. But I should have thought you might want to come out sooner when your only daughter is back from a six-month visit.

GODWIN. Mary understands.

MARY. Of course I do.

GODWIN. And I had three daughters last time I looked.

MRS GODWIN. You know very well what I mean – the only one as is the fruit of your loins.

JANE. Maman, must you? Must you use such awful words?

MRS GODWIN. Oh, don't you start that.

JANE. What?

MRS GODWIN. You've been doing it all day – making out there's some sort of coarseness in me which you don't like to be associated with.

JANE. I've done nothing of the sort.

MRS GODWIN. A few weeks at boarding school and you think you can look down on me. Well, you can't.

JANE. But…

MRS GODWIN. I'm just as good as you – (*Pointing at* MARY.) and you, and I shan't be treated like this in my own home.

JANE. Maman, I didn't mean anything. Really…

MRS GODWIN. Loins is a perfectly respectable word. I'm sure it is in Mr Johnson's Dictionary. I'm sure everyone has loins. Do you have loins, Mr Godwin?

GODWIN. I'm rather afraid I do.

MRS GODWIN. There. And I'm sure most people would be happy to admit to it.

FANNY *enters, carrying a tray of tea things*.

FANNY. I didn't get an answer, Jane.

JANE. Oh, sorry, Fanny. I forgot.

MRS GODWIN. One each. One each.

FANNY. Good. That's what I thought.

MARY. We're not elephants.

FANNY *carries the tray to the table*.

MRS GODWIN. Bring your chair round, Mary. Don't just stand there.

JANE. Who are they hanging, Papa? Do you know?

GODWIN. A man called Bates. Theft of a gun.

FANNY. Shall I go down and sit in the shop?

MARY. No, Fanny.

MRS GODWIN. Oh, I've closed the shop. We shan't get any customers now with this going on. I always said this was a stupid place to open a children's bookshop. We're so close to the gallows we can almost hear the necks snap.

JANE. Maman!

MARY. At least we get passing trade.

MRS GODWIN. Oh, yes. I'm sure any number of these louts is likely to pop in for a copy of *Pilgrim's Progress*.

GODWIN. I don't remember you saying this was a stupid place to open a bookshop, Mrs Godwin.

MRS GODWIN. Well, that just shows how seldom you listen to me.

Oh, do come away and sit down, Jane. Let's all just sit down nicely and have tea, like normal people.

They sit together, and tea commences. In the street below, someone in the passing crowd is shouting, and there is a burst of laughter. GODWIN *raises his teacup to* MARY.

GODWIN. Welcome home, Mary.

MARY. Thank you.

JANE. Yes. Welcome home.

GODWIN. How was the dreaded voyage?

MARY. It passed quite quickly. And the weather was so beautiful this morning. I was on deck to see the sun rise.

GODWIN. You look well, at any rate. The Scottish air obviously agreed with you.

MARY. It did.

MRS GODWIN. She didn't see Charles.

GODWIN. And a new dress, eh?

MARY. Yes. Thank you for sending the money.

GODWIN. You put me in mind of one of Walter Scott's heroines.

JANE. I've never been sure about tartan. I mean, I'm sure it looks very fine in its natural… habitat, as it were. The Highlands, and the glens. Kilts, and so on.

FANNY. I think it's a very pretty dress.

JANE. Oh, so do I. In fact, I should love to have one just like it.

MRS GODWIN. You've had your new dress this season.

JANE. Yes, I know. I only meant…

She trails off.

GODWIN. And how did you spend your days?

MARY. Walking, mostly. Bathing a little. Though the water was ferociously cold.

MRS GODWIN. The Baxters send their regards. Evidently.

MARY. I have letters for you from Mr Baxter, Papa.

MRS GODWIN. Letters. Oh. Very nice.

GODWIN. Thank you.

And I hope you did some writing.

MARY. I did. I've begun a new story.

FANNY. What's it about?

MARY. It's about… But I won't say yet. Because I'm not quite sure if it's going to take. You understand.

GODWIN. Only too well.

MARY. But when I've finished it, I'll show it to Papa, and if he thinks it's good enough, I shall read it to you all.

MRS GODWIN. I have begun a new translation – *The Swiss Family Robinson*. It is very taxing.

JANE. Did Fanny tell you about Mr Shelley, Mary?

MARY. Yes.

JANE. I can't wait for you to meet him.

MARY. You've met him already?

JANE. He was here yesterday. And he really is the most extraordinary man. Quite the most… vibrant human being I have ever met.

GODWIN. Yes. I'm afraid you will find that both your sisters are rather taken with my young friend Shelley.

FANNY. Papa, really.

JANE. Is he coming this evening?

GODWIN. Tomorrow.

MARY. He's doing some business with you – is that right?

GODWIN. Of sorts. I am helping him with a rather complicated financial transaction, and he is showing a kind interest in our little enterprise here.

JANE. He's giving Papa some money.

GODWIN. Lending me some money, Jane. Lending me some money so that I might be able to discharge one or two of the difficulties which have built up of late, and so that I might begin to concentrate on my writing again. Which is the most important thing.

MARY. Yes.

MRS GODWIN. Well, I shall believe it when I see it. I wouldn't be at all surprised if we never saw a penny of this alleged money from Mr Shelley.

JANE. Maman.

MARY. Why?

MRS GODWIN. Firstly, because he doesn't have any money.
He's having to borrow it himself, against his future fortune…

GODWIN. I would rather we didn't speak of business at tea.

MRS GODWIN.…at an exorbitant cost. And secondly, because
the only reliable thing about Mr Shelley is that he is
completely unreliable. He turns up here when he isn't
invited, and then when he is invited, he doesn't turn up. I've
lost count of the number of dinners I've prepared for him,
only to have them wasted.

GODWIN. You cannot dismiss a man's character on the basis
of a few discarded chops.

MRS GODWIN. Chops which have to be paid for, and with
money we haven't got. And then there was the time he
disappeared altogether. What's to stop him doing that again?

FANNY. That was a long time ago, Mama.

MRS GODWIN. And what of that?

FANNY. I… I think he's become more reliable lately. I think…

MRS GODWIN. 'Come to my hotel, Mrs Godwin. Dine with
us, Mr Godwin.' And then we get there and he's gone.
Packed up and left. I've never been so humiliated.

MARY. Do we need the money badly, Papa?

GODWIN. There is no question of Shelley disappearing. I have
great faith in him. You cannot sit for hours with a man,
discussing my *Political Justice* without learning something
of his true nature. There are certain principles upon which
we disagree, yes, but he knows as well as I what constitutes
just treatment of one man by another. Now can we please
stop discussing business at tea.

MRS GODWIN. You are too trusting, Mr Godwin.

GODWIN. And you are too cynical, my dear.

MRS GODWIN. I'd rather be cynical than an old fool.

There is a moment of shocked silence.

MARY. It's possible to be both. It's possible to be a cynical old fool.

FANNY. Mary…

MARY. I only said it's possible.

MRS GODWIN. Is that in some way directed at me?

(*To* GODWIN.) Are you going to let her speak to me like that?

GODWIN. I'm sorry, I must have missed that.

MRS GODWIN. Oh, I see. Return of the selective deafness.

GODWIN. Now, now, my dear.

MARY. I also did a great deal of reading in Scotland.

GODWIN. I hope you kept a list.

MARY. I did. *Clarissa*…

GODWIN. Ah, yes.

MARY. And I read your memoir of my mother. (*Looking at* FANNY.) Of our mother. *Memoirs of the Author of the Rights of Woman*.

GODWIN. Did you?

MRS GODWIN. You read the *Memoirs*?

GODWIN. First or second edition?

MARY. First.

MRS GODWIN. Is that all you've got to say?

MARY. It's a beautiful piece of writing, Papa. Aside from anything else. I couldn't be more proud of you. Or of my wonderful mother.

GODWIN. Yes. I see. I am gratified.

JANE. What memoir?

MARY. A memoir of Mary Wollstonecraft. Papa tells the whole story of her life. Her politics, her philosophies, her travels. Her love affairs.

MRS GODWIN. Well. I suppose I am expected to keep quiet on this occasion. But I must say, I shouldn't have thought it suitable reading at all for a sixteen-year-old girl.

MARY. Why not? I think it should be compulsory reading for all sixteen-year-old girls. To learn about such a woman. So courageous. So liberated.

MRS GODWIN. Well, I don't want Jane reading it.

JANE. Maman!

MARY. Why not?

FANNY. I think we should change the subject.

MARY. Why don't you wish Jane to read it?

MRS GODWIN. Oh, I couldn't possibly say. Because it's none of my business, is it?

MARY. No, it isn't. It isn't any of your business.

GODWIN. Mary…

MRS GODWIN. How dare you speak to me like that?

MARY. I do dare. I suppose you're going to threaten to slap my wrists? Send me to bed without any supper? I came back here determined to be civil to you but it is impossible. No one in the whole of Scotland ever spoke to me in such a rude and disrespectful way.

MRS GODWIN. Disrespectful? Huh! That's very high and mighty, I must say.

MARY. The Baxters did not even speak to their dogs in such a way!

GODWIN (*standing*). Time to get back to work, everyone. I'm sure we all have things we should be doing.

MRS GODWIN. Oh, that's right, Mr Godwin – run off back to your study.

The noise of a great roar from the nearby crowd is heard. JANE rushes to the window.

MARY. So rude!

GODWIN. Please attempt to control your temper, Mrs Godwin. Remember what we spoke about.

JANE *bursts into tears*.

MRS GODWIN. What's the matter with you?

JANE. He's dead.

MRS GODWIN. Who is?

JANE. The poor man. All he did was steal a gun and now he's dead, dead, dead.

MRS GODWIN. Well, he was nothing to you, you silly girl.

JANE. He was a fellow creature. A fellow creature and now he's dead.

MARY (*going to leave*). I've had enough of this.

MRS GODWIN. Don't you think of flouncing out. If anyone is going to flounce out, it's me!

MRS GODWIN *leaves*. JANE *sobs loudly*.

GODWIN. Well. Thank you for tea.

GODWIN *exits to the study*.

FANNY. Mary, did you have to?

MARY. Yes. Yes, I did.

Scene Four

Evening. GODWIN*'s study. Windows look out onto the street. Above a large fireplace there is a portrait of Mary Wollstonecraft. Books line the walls, and lie in piles on the floor. Between the windows there is an old leather sofa.* GODWIN *is working at his desk.* MARY *enters quietly. There is a small bundle of letters in her hand.*

MARY. The letters from Mr Baxter, Papa.

GODWIN (*without looking up*). Thank you. Place them there.

MARY *puts them on the desk. She waits, but he continues to work.*

MARY. Shouldn't you stop now? It's quite late.

GODWIN. One or two things more.

MARY. What are you working on?

GODWIN. It doesn't deserve to be called work. Calculations. Business. Commercial drudgery.

MARY. All the more reason to stop.

She goes to stand before the portrait and stares up at it.

How old was she in this portrait?

GODWIN. About thirty-eight. She was pregnant with you.

MARY. She looks content.

GODWIN. You have grown more like her.

MARY. Have I?

GODWIN. A little in your looks. A great deal in your stridency of expression.

You went away a girl, and have returned a young woman.

GODWIN *finishes his work and sets his pen down. They smile at each other.*

So, am I forgiven for sending you away?

MARY. I wasn't cross. Just a little nervous, I suppose.

GODWIN. I knew it was time for you to make a foray into the outside world.

MARY. You were right.

GODWIN. Your mother was a great believer in girls experiencing life outside the home. Within reason, of course.

MARY. Papa, are there more books about my mother which I can read? Or can I read the other books she wrote?

GODWIN. Hum. I can't remember what you've read already.

He goes to the bookshelves.

MARY. Not that much. *The Rights of Woman*. You read us that. *View of the French Revolution*.

GODWIN. Her travels in Sweden?

MARY. No.

He hands it to her.

GODWIN. I think Fanny has read that one. Of course, there's a great deal in there about Fanny, as a baby. Your mother took her with her on her travels.

MARY. Yes. Anything else?

GODWIN (*hesitating*). There are the letters.

MARY. The letters?

GODWIN. I edited a volume of her letters. But perhaps that's for another day.

MARY. Please let me see it. I feel as though I've been sleeping on top of buried treasure.

GODWIN (*handing it to her*). Very well.

MARY. Thank you.

GODWIN. Mary…

MARY. I'm sorry I lost my temper with Mrs Godwin. But she seemed to be implying that there was something wrong about my mother – about the way she lived. And there wasn't, was there?

GODWIN. No. But, Mary, you are old enough to understand now that there are many people who cannot view the world as openly as your mother did. Or as you and I do.

MARY. You mean small-minded people. Like Mrs Godwin.

GODWIN. That is not what I mean.

MARY. But she spoke about your book as though it were contaminated.

GODWIN. Mrs Godwin has worked hard – tremendously hard, as have I, to achieve the relatively settled life which we have given you. And all our children. If she is a little alarmed, or decidedly averse to anything which seems to… veer towards scandal, then she is understandably so.

MARY. Scandal?

GODWIN. The *Memoirs* were not well received. It is only right that you be made aware of that.

In fact, I was vilified.

MARY. But…

GODWIN. And not only in the reactionary press. Some people – friends even – thought I was wrong to write in detail about her private affairs. Some thought I was wrong to write so quickly after her death. I was only trying to make something useful out of tragedy…

MARY. Yes.

GODWIN. But I was judged – we were both judged, very harshly. The suicide attempt… the circumstances of Fanny's birth… many people thought I should have left those things unstated. It was a shock to me. I had not realised until then how entirely out of step I had become – even with radical society.

In the second edition, I tried to remedy some of the damage. Her sisters in Ireland – your aunts – had been very upset by the book. One or two of her friends…

MARY. But you don't regret writing it? Surely you don't.

GODWIN. No. Although, in hindsight, I am not at all sure that I should have had it published.

MARY. But surely for every person who balked at it, there was someone like me… who found it inspiring?

GODWIN. I simply want you to be aware that there are certain sensitivities surrounding your mother's reputation, which we must be mindful of. Not least because we are reliant upon a business. A shop which sells books for children.

MARY. Then perhaps we should not be. If it means we cannot be true to our principles and to your philosophies. If it means I cannot be openly proud of my mother.

GODWIN. Well. I'm afraid we must deal with things as they are.

Come and kiss me.

She does so. She hugs him.

MARY. Poor Papa.

GODWIN. You even smell the way your mother used to smell. Is that possible, do you think?

MARY. I'm sure it is.

GODWIN. My dearest girl.

You are right to be proud of your mother, Mary. But we must be patient, cautious with those who do not have our capacity and strength of mind. Always remember who you are. And ask more of yourself.

Goodnight now.

MARY. Goodnight.

She starts to go.

I wish she hadn't died. I wish we were together now. My mother and you. Fanny and I. That was how it was meant to be.

She leaves.

Scene Five

Late at night. GODWIN's study.

There is the sound of knocking on the front door of the house. It stops. After a few moments, GODWIN enters, with SHELLEY behind him. GODWIN is carrying a candle.

GODWIN. We had better come in here.

SHELLEY. I didn't realise it was so late.

GODWIN *lights a lamp*.

You weren't in bed?

GODWIN. Yes. But no matter.

SHELLEY. Was I expected here this evening? I felt sure I was.

GODWIN. We expected you tomorrow, Shelley.

SHELLEY. Ah. Tomorrow. Then I'm early.

GODWIN. Yes. Early and late, it would seem. A walking challenge to the laws of physics.

SHELLEY. I went to the Fleet this afternoon. The first time I've been in a prison. It shook me rather.

GODWIN. I'm sure it did.

SHELLEY. I went for a walk by the river. I must have lost track of time. And the days are getting longer now, aren't they? Perhaps it was that. A trick of the light.

GODWIN. What took you to the Fleet? Sit down for a moment.

SHELLEY. A friend of mine was arrested for debt yesterday. He has a wife and five children to support.

GODWIN. I'm sorry to hear it.

SHELLEY. It's the perversity of it which enrages me. To confine a man, to shackle him, at the very moment he has most need to be industrious.

GODWIN. Does your friend have private rooms, at least?

SHELLEY. No, no. He shares a cell with three others. I thought I knew what it was to be in prison. But the reality... I took him a copy of *Caleb Williams*.

GODWIN. Did you?

SHELLEY. He had read it, of course, but he was glad to have it with him. A lone voice of sanity amidst the madness. 'Go, go, ignorant fool and visit the scenes of our prisons, then show me the man shameless enough to rejoice and say, "England has no Bastille".'

GODWIN. Yes. Those passages were the result of bitter experience. I dare not think of the hours I have spent visiting men in prison cells. Good men. Wasted lives.

SHELLEY. I am going to take up the cry. I don't know how yet, but I shall. Godwin, when will we have the money? I have sworn that I will help him. I won't use any of your share, of course, but I shall use mine – all of it, if need be.

GODWIN. We are making progress, certainly. I saw the lawyers this afternoon.

SHELLEY. What did they say?

FANNY *enters. She is in a nightdress and dressing gown.*

FANNY. Oh. Mr Shelley.

SHELLEY. Miss Godwin. Forgive me. I have come rather…

GODWIN. Early.

SHELLEY. Yes.

FANNY. Please don't worry. I only wondered if anyone had need of anything. Are you staying, Mr Shelley?

SHELLEY. Staying? Yes. Yes. Thank you. If that would be agreeable?

GODWIN. By all means, stay a while.

SHELLEY. It's true I have no wish to be alone tonight. If I could lie down amongst friends it would mean a great deal to me.

FANNY. Oh.

GODWIN. Ah. Staying.

SHELLEY. It has been a day of great emotion.

FANNY. Yes. I must see if the spare room is… Sometimes it is rather full of books and so on.

SHELLEY. But I can sleep in here. If you don't object, Godwin?

GODWIN. No.

SHELLEY. When I get tired I can sleep anywhere. I shall sleep curled up on the rug there. Or on the sofa.

FANNY. Yes.

SHELLEY. A blanket, perhaps, for the early hours? And a glass of water, please. If it isn't too much trouble.

FANNY. Not at all. I'll fetch them.

SHELLEY. Thank you.

FANNY *leaves*. GODWIN *and* SHELLEY *sit down together.*

GODWIN. I was imprisoned once. For debt. Did I tell you that?

SHELLEY. No.

GODWIN. In the early days. When I was trying to make my way. People assume that philosophers can live on air. My friends and I were completely reliant upon one another. If one of us went under, another would always try to help him out.

SHELLEY. That's how it should be.

GODWIN. Nothing has changed really. Except these days there are a great many noughts on the amounts which we owe.

SHELLEY. What did the lawyers say?

GODWIN. Yes. So. It seems the purchasers of the bond are now satisfied on the question of life insurance.

SHELLEY. Good.

GODWIN. But they have now come back with two further questions. The first concerns existing borrowing against the estate. They wish to be certain that when your grandfather dies, they will not find that there are prior and sweeping claims upon his property and land.

SHELLEY. How absurd this is.

GODWIN. Do you know if your grandfather has borrowed against the estate?

SHELLEY. I'm quite sure he hasn't.

GODWIN. And your father?

SHELLEY. No. He is entirely opposed to borrowing. It's one of the reasons why he is entirely opposed to me.

GODWIN. With your permission, I will write to your family's lawyer to ask for a statement on the subject.

SHELLEY. How long will that take?

GODWIN. I can't say exactly. We could consider a direct approach to your grandfather, but...

SHELLEY. What is the matter with these people? If they didn't want to buy the bond, why did they bid for it? They're already getting it for a lot less than it is worth. Surely they should understand that there is some risk attached to it?

GODWIN. No one was prepared to bid higher. We must remember that.

Do not be disheartened. We're drawing close now.

SHELLEY. What is the second question?

GODWIN. I think we should leave that for the morning. We can talk before breakfast, if you prefer.

SHELLEY. Please, Godwin. I am not a 'wait until the morning' sort of person.

GODWIN. As you wish. It concerns your marriage.

SHELLEY. My marriage?

GODWIN. They are not convinced that your existing certificate of marriage would stand up to scrutiny in an English court. If you were to die, and there were any challenges to the legitimacy of your heirs, their claim could stall – or be rejected completely.

SHELLEY. I don't understand.

GODWIN. You were married in Scotland, I think? In some form of chapel?

SHELLEY. Yes. We eloped.

GODWIN. Well, what they are asking is that you marry again. In an English church. In the Church of England.

Do you foresee any difficulty with that?

Will Mrs Shelley be in London at all this week?

SHELLEY. No. She is staying in Windsor with the baby.

GODWIN. Then could you arrange to be married there? Tomorrow, I can accompany you to get a certificate. You could consider a marriage the following day. And if you have need of witnesses…

SHELLEY. You know my views on marriage, Godwin. They are the same as yours. They were forged by you.

GODWIN. Yes. And yet we both sit here, married men.

SHELLEY. I married in haste. I could see no other way of protecting Harriet.

GODWIN. Precisely.

SHELLEY. I was young then.

GODWIN. Really, Shelley…

SHELLEY. It did not seem too abhorrent, to stand in a chapel and make some vows. It did not even seem like a church. To do so again – in cold blood. I don't think I can.

I'm sorry. They will have to accept my marriage as it is.

They are quiet for a moment.

GODWIN. We must apply philosophy to this situation. Once you have the money – we have the money – the use we can make of it will far outweigh the small but necessary evil of your repeating your wedding vows. We must use convention to defeat convention.

The alternative is… what? That we lose the sale. I need not tell you, I think, the consequences that would have.

I sympathise. Believe me. Sometimes, when I look back on my own life, it seems…

SHELLEY. What?

GODWIN. One learns to live with compromise. A horrible bed-bound relative in a secret room.

Pause.

SHELLEY. I will speak to Harriet.

GODWIN. Yes.

SHELLEY. Though I do not feel at all comfortable about doing so. Our relations at present would not naturally tend towards a renewal of vows. In fact…

MRS GODWIN *is heard from outside the door –*

MRS GODWIN (*off*). Mr Godwin? What is going on?

GODWIN (*to* SHELLEY). Excuse me one moment?

GODWIN *leaves. There is the sound of whispering. After a moment,* FANNY *enters. She is carrying some blankets and a glass of water.*

SHELLEY. I appear to have woken the whole house.

FANNY. Don't worry.

FANNY *begins to make up a bed on the sofa.*

I think you should sleep on here tonight. Please don't sleep on the floor.

SHELLEY. If anyone had told me, when I was at school, that one day I would lie down to sleep in the study of the great William Godwin – with Mary Wollstonecraft gazing down upon me – I would have thought it too much a fantasy to be believed. And to have her legendary daughter as my companion…

FANNY. I am hardly legendary.

SHELLEY. But you are. You must know you are. No child has ever been so lovingly described. Your joy in being, your inquisitiveness.

FANNY. I am glad to have those descriptions to look back upon.

SHELLEY. You know, when Harriet first discovered she was pregnant, I gave her a copy of your mother's thoughts on raising daughters. In case we had a girl. And then we did –

FANNY. Has she found it useful?

SHELLEY. Yes. Though she has not taken it to heart entirely – in the way I hoped she would. On education she is completely agreed. But she would not feed the baby herself. That I found very difficult. She hired a wet nurse. I would have snatched the child away and fed her myself if I could.

FANNY. I'm sorry. I suppose it is a very personal… It's very personal.

SHELLEY. Yes.

FANNY. But your daughter is well, isn't she?

SHELLEY. Yes. She is thriving.

FANNY. That's the most important thing. I feel sure my mother would say so.

SHELLEY. We are to have another. Harriet told me this morning.

FANNY. Oh. Another baby.

SHELLEY. Some time in the autumn.

FANNY. That's wonderful. That's wonderful news.

SHELLEY. I suppose it is.

FANNY. You aren't sure?

SHELLEY. It's very hard… this question of responsibility… to one's own children. I wish… I want to take responsibility for the whole world, and yet I am expected to reserve a vast share of my attention for one or two individual creatures, whom I had a part in creating. Do you understand what I mean?

FANNY. I think I do.

SHELLEY. Today… I saw a small boy being thrown into the river.

FANNY. Oh, no.

SHELLEY. He was on a coal barge that was passing by. He was arguing with a large man. And the man suddenly picked him up and tossed him over the side. Quite casually. As though he were emptying his piss-pot. The boy was floundering. I ran down to the edge of the water and made as much commotion as I could. I can't swim, or I would have gone in to get him.

FANNY. Yes.

SHELLEY. He was picked up and rowed to shore. I felt so much for him. I wanted to keep him.

I would have taken him home, but all he wanted was to run to catch up with the barge. I gave him all the money in my pockets. I felt so much for him, in his plight. As much as I have ever felt for my own child. Does that seem wrong?

FANNY. No. No, not at all. I have often felt quite overwhelmed with love for the children I visit in the poor schools.

SHELLEY. Have you?

FANNY. I have often thought there could be no greater vocation in life – no greater use of energy – than to rescue a whole class full of those children from the evils of poverty and ignorance.

SHELLEY. A greater vocation than motherhood?

FANNY. Yes.

SHELLEY. How right you are. How wise.

Why don't you stay with me, and talk to me all night? Really. I don't feel at all sleepy. Do you?

FANNY. No, but… I would like to, but…

SHELLEY. But what? Have you ever stayed up and talked all night?

FANNY. No…

SHELLEY. Then you must. It is one of the great pleasures of life.

FANNY. I don't think… I don't think Mama would allow it.

SHELLEY. Why not? Would you stay if I were a woman?

FANNY. Yes.

SHELLEY. Then stay. Surely your father, of all people, would not insist upon the proprieties?

Are we such animals that we cannot control our desires?

FANNY *cannot answer.* GODWIN *enters.*

FANNY. I'll say goodnight.

GODWIN. Yes.

FANNY (*to* SHELLEY). Goodnight.

SHELLEY. If goodnight it must be.

She leaves. He gazes after her.

Scene Six

Morning. GODWIN*'s study.* SHELLEY *is lying on the sofa under a blanket. The sounds of the busy street below are drifting into the room.*

MARY *enters. She is wearing a dressing gown, and her hair is undone. She does not see* SHELLEY. *She heads towards her father's desk, but then changes her mind and goes to the window and draws back the curtains.*

SHELLEY. But soft, what light through yonder window breaks?

MARY *gasps with surprise.* SHELLEY *sits up, smiling. He is in a state of half-undress.*

Sorry. I couldn't resist… Oh.

MARY. I didn't realise there was anyone in here.

SHELLEY. I'm sorry. I thought you were Miss Godwin.

I stayed the night.

Shelley. Percy. Bysshe.

MARY. Ah. Of course.

SHELLEY. And you? Are you…?

MARY. Mary. Mary Wollstonecraft Godwin.

SHELLEY. Mary. You're back.

MARY. Yes.

SHELLEY. No one told me.

The immediate rapport between them is tangible.

MARY. I'll go and tell Mrs Godwin you're awake.

She starts to go.

SHELLEY. But what did you come for?

MARY. Oh. It doesn't matter.

SHELLEY. A book? I would be the last person on earth to deprive you of a book.

MARY. I came for some paper.

SHELLEY (*jumping up*). Paper! Let me help you find some.

MARY. It's all right. I think I know where it is. My notebook's full, and I just need a few sheets of paper, until I can get another one.

SHELLEY. Are you writing? Your sisters told me that you write. You cannot know how happy I was to hear that. What are you writing?

MARY. A story.

SHELLEY. I write poetry.

MARY. Do you?

SHELLEY. Yes. I have recently finished a poem. It's my best work. I have had several copies printed.

MARY. That's wonderful.

SHELLEY. Yes. It's a long poem. Epic, I suppose one could say. I can't put my name to it – the content is too dangerous. It's not that I'm afraid to take on the authorities. But I don't want to find myself in prison when I've only just begun.

MARY. What's it about?

SHELLEY. It is very much inspired by your father's work.

MARY. Is it really?

SHELLEY. Although I showed it to him and he was rather critical. He thinks I should stick to prose. Prose and politics.

MARY. But my father has never been fond of poetry. You ought to hear him on the subject of Lord Byron.

SHELLEY. Really? I adore Byron.

MARY. So do I. But Father likes things to be said in a… logical way. I'm sure it is not the fault of your poem.

JANE *enters*.

JANE. Oh. Mary. You're here.

MARY. Good morning, Jane.

SHELLEY. Miss Jane! How sweet and fresh you look today.

JANE. Do I? I've only just woken up.

But look at you two. You've met at last.

SHELLEY. Yes.

JANE. It's not fair. It's really too unkind. I wanted to be the person to introduce you. I told him all about you, Mary. Now, is she as lovely as I said she is?

MARY. Jane.

SHELLEY. Certainly, she is.

MARY. Jane, please.

JANE. What?

MARY. Please don't say such silly things.

JANE. Oh, don't be embarrassed. Embarrassment is so petty. But, Shelley, I must tell you something quite extraordinary.

SHELLEY. That's a very promising beginning.

JANE. When Mama told me just now that you had stayed the night, I wasn't at all surprised, because I knew. Because all night… all night I had the strangest feeling that you were close by.

SHELLEY. Did you really?

JANE. I was finding it hard to sleep, you see, because I had been so upset yesterday about the poor man being hanged. Hadn't I, Mary? I was quite inconsolable. I can't bear any sort of cruelty, can I, Mary?

MARY. No.

JANE. But then I started to feel quite calm suddenly, and I started to feel that there was a presence close by – a good, strong presence – and then I realised that it was you.

SHELLEY. That's fascinating.

JANE. And then I slept quite happily. And calmly. How can I describe it? I felt very… soft. And relaxed.

SHELLEY. How extraordinary. I'm glad to have been of service.

JANE (*laughing*). Did you know? I mean, were you… thinking…?

SHELLEY. I wasn't conscious of anything.

JANE. You didn't come upstairs at all?

SHELLEY. No. But who knows where our souls wander when we sleep?

GODWIN *enters and goes straight to his desk*.

GODWIN. Ah, you're awake, Shelley. Good. (*Calling*.) Fanny! She was afraid we might disturb you, but I see we are too late for that.

JANE. He was awake when I came in, Papa.

GODWIN (*to* MARY *and* SHELLEY). So you've met.

SHELLEY. Yes. We introduced ourselves.

FANNY *enters*.

FANNY. Good morning.

SHELLEY. Good morning, my dear Miss Godwin.

FANNY. Rather an invasion, I'm afraid. Would you like a little privacy?

SHELLEY. No. This is the perfect start to my day.

FANNY. How are you, Mary? Rested?

MARY. Yes, thank you, dear.

GODWIN. This is the letter I wish you to copy, Fanny.

FANNY (*crossing to the desk*). Jane, go down and mind the shop please.

JANE. Now?

FANNY. Yes.

JANE. But I don't want to. Surely if anyone comes they can ring the bell? No one will come anyway.

GODWIN. Will it be clear enough?

FANNY. Yes. I think so.

GODWIN. Shelley, I've ascertained where we must go for the certificate, but the office will close at midday, so we must start out as soon as you're ready.

SHELLEY. Right. Yes. What time is it now?

MARY. It's almost half-past ten.

SHELLEY. Is it really?

JANE. I'm always losing track of time.

MRS GODWIN *enters*.

MRS GODWIN. What on earth is going on in here?

I do apologise, Mr Shelley. I gave orders that you were not to be disturbed.

JANE. Mary was here before I was.

SHELLEY. But it's been splendid, Mrs Godwin. Really. It reminds me of being a child again. Waking up surrounded by my sisters.

MRS GODWIN. Well, we are none of us children now. What do you say, Mr Godwin?

GODWIN. What's that, my dear?

MRS GODWIN. Come out now, girls. In fact, no. Mr Shelley, I think you should come out, if you don't mind? You may use my bedroom in which to refresh yourself, and so forth. I'm sure you must need to do that.

SHELLEY. Thank you. You're very kind.

MRS GODWIN. And who's minding the shop, may I ask?

FANNY. I was. But I'm busy now. I asked Jane to go down.

MRS GODWIN. Then go down, Jane. At once. What do you think this is? A public holiday?

JANE (*to* SHELLEY). Will you be coming back?

SHELLEY. I hope so. Will we come back, Godwin?

GODWIN. Back? No. Windsor.

SHELLEY. Ah, yes. A pity.

JANE. But you'll come again soon?

MRS GODWIN. Jane!

JANE. Sorry. (*To* SHELLEY.) Come out through the shop and say goodbye!

She leaves.

MRS GODWIN (*inviting him to come with her*). Mr Shelley?

SHELLEY (*to* MARY). I hope I will see you soon. You're not going away again?

MARY. No. I have no more plans to travel.

SHELLEY. I wonder if you would read my poem? Would you?

MARY. Yes. Of course. I would like that very much.

SHELLEY. I will come back as soon as I can.

They smile deeply at each other.

Good day, Miss Godwin.

FANNY. Good day. I hope…

MRS GODWIN (*ushering him out*). I have saved you a nice slice of bacon for your breakfast, Mr Shelley.

GODWIN. No time!

SHELLEY. Oh, I never eat breakfast, Mrs Godwin. Or meat.

MRS GODWIN. No? Of course you don't.

They leave.

GODWIN. Right. Once you have finished it, I want you to deliver it. You know the office?

FANNY. Yes, Papa.

GODWIN. As soon as you can.

He gathers his things together.

Writing today, Mary?

MARY. Yes, Papa.

GODWIN. Very good.

He leaves. FANNY watches MARY for a moment. MARY is looking shocked and flushed.

FANNY. So… That is Mr Shelley.

MARY. Yes.

I need some paper.

MARY goes to the desk and finds the paper.

FANNY. Is something wrong?

MARY. No. Not at all.

FANNY. What did you think of him?

MARY. I thought he was… Yes. He's very pleasant.

FANNY. 'Pleasant'? What do you mean? That's the most… pale… the most insipid word I ever heard fall from your lips.

MARY. He's beautiful. There must be angels who command less light.

Looking at MARY's impassioned face, FANNY is suddenly filled with disquiet. MARY sees it.

You looked after him last night?

FANNY. Yes. We had a long talk.

MARY. I'm glad. Well. I'll let you get on. Tell me if I can be of any help.

FANNY. Yes. Thank you.

MARY leaves.

Scene Seven

The sisters' bedroom. MARY rushes in. She is full of the most staggering emotions – literally lovestruck. She feels as though the room is too small to contain her. She throws the pieces of paper up into the air.

She sits down suddenly, hugging her knees and covering her mouth. Then she laughs.

MARY. Madness.

She stands again. She has to move, to release the feeling.

I wonder if you would read my poem? Would you?

Yes. Of course. Of course. Of course. Of course.

I will come back as soon as I can.

Come back. Come back to me. Mr Shelley. Shelley. Like the name of a rose. Or something fragile from the sea.

Scene Eight

Night. The sisters' bedroom. MARY, in her nightgown, pulls all the blankets and quilts from the beds into the middle of the floor. She lights candles and places them around. She takes the books she has borrowed from her father, and places them on the covers.

She goes to the window and opens it, letting the moonlight in.

MARY. Come, gentle night; come, loving black-brow'd night.

FANNY enters. She is in her nightgown and carries a candle. She stops in astonishment – a little thrilled by the sight.

FANNY. Mary? What…?

MARY takes FANNY's hand and sits her on the covers.

MARY. I have more books. Love letters. More beautiful than you can imagine. Papa gave them to me, so you need not fear.

FANNY (*looking at the little book of letters*). I don't know if I can.

MARY. We have to. Mother may not be here, but she can still teach us what it is to love.

She takes the book and goes to a marked page.

Look – read this page.

FANNY takes it and reads.

Read it aloud.

FANNY (*reading*). 'I have been playing and laughing with the little girl so long, that I cannot take up my pen to address you without emotion.'

MARY. It is written to your father – do you see?

FANNY (*reading*). 'Pressing her to my bosom, she looked so like you, every nerve seemed to vibrate to the touch, and you seemed to pervade my whole frame, quickening the beat of my heart.' The child is me.

MARY. Yes.

JANE enters, also dressed for bed and carrying a candle.

JANE. What are you doing?

MARY. Hush, Jane. Come away from the door.

JANE. What are you doing? Can I join in?

She sits with them on the floor. She picks up a book.

Ah! Is this it? Is this the *Memoir*?

MARY (*reading*). 'Recollection now makes my heart bound to thee; I have thy honest countenance before me, relaxed by tenderness. Thy lips then feel softer than soft, and I rest my cheek on thine, forgetting all the world.'

JANE. But that is too gorgeous!

FANNY. Is that written to my father too?

MARY. She must have loved him deeply. I'm sure, when we were younger, we were made to think it was no more than a passing fancy.

JANE. Listen to this. (*Reading from the* Memoirs.) 'Mary rested her head upon my shoulder – the shoulder of her lover…' This is Papa speaking!

FANNY. Papa?

JANE (*reading*). '…I had never loved till now; or, at least, had never nourished a passion to the same growth, or met with an object so consummately worthy.' Is that not the funniest thing?

MARY. That is Papa's way of saying that he was overwhelmed with passion!

She throws herself onto JANE, *who laughs*.

Abandoned to a desire that changed him utterly, that pushed him to the ground, that launched him to the winds!

FANNY (*reading from the* Memoirs). 'We did not marry.' I thought they did.

MARY. Eventually. But I was conceived in the first throes of their passion.

JANE. Oh, Mary!

FANNY. You don't mind, do you?

MARY. Of course not. Marriage is a nonsense. You were conceived at a tollgate, Fanny.

JANE. A tollgate?

MARY (*taking up the* Letters). Look here – let me see… here. She calls you her 'barrier-girl'. She would meet your father at one of the barriers into Paris.

FANNY. 'Barrier-girl'? Papa used to call me the barrier-child sometimes. Do you remember? I always thought it meant something bad. That I had been in the way somehow.

MARY. Oh, Fanny. They would spend nights together in a room in the tollgate.

JANE. How romantic!

FANNY. Is that really true?

MARY. A child of the Revolution.

JANE. And outside, all around, people were having their heads chopped off!

MARY. Look here – (*Reading*.) '…my imagination then rather chooses to ramble back to the barrier with you, to see you coming to meet me, and my basket of grapes and wine, and with the blissful hours to come.'

JANE. I never heard of anything so romantic.

They lie back and grow quieter. FANNY *reads to the end of the letter.*

FANNY. 'My little barrier-girl…'

JANE. I wish she was my mother. Oh, I wish she was.

I am going to change my name to hers. Jane is such a dull name. And really I was christened Mary-Jane, so…

FANNY (*laughing*). But you can't take 'Mary'.

JANE. Oh, yes! Oh, no. Then I shall take her birthday! When was her birthday?

FANNY. April the twenty-seventh.

JANE. Then from now on that will be my birthday. Will you let me? And you must mark it.

You will, won't you?

MARY. All right.

JANE. But don't tell Mama, or she will laugh and think me stupid.

FANNY. Let's blow out the candles now.

They do so, and settle down.

MARY. We cannot let our lives be small. There is no life but loving.

Gradually, they begin to drift into sleep. In MARY's *mind,* SHELLEY *enters the room. The energy between them draws them together. They do not touch, but seem to lean and brush against each other.*

When she awakens, FANNY *is standing by the window, gazing out at the night sky.*

(*Whispering.*) Are you all right, Fanny?

FANNY. It is too much to bear.

MARY (*hesitantly*). What do you mean?

But FANNY *only goes back to her bed and closes her eyes.*

End of Act One.

ACT TWO

Scene One

St Pancras Churchyard. Bright sunshine filtered through trees. One large tomb – that of Mary Wollstonecraft – dominates the space. JANE runs up to it, and sits upon it, arranging her skirts and hair to their full advantage.

MARY and SHELLEY appear from the same direction. They are deep in discussion.

SHELLEY. All established religions work hand in hand with tyranny. They dull men's minds. They stop us from thinking we can make our own moral choices.

MARY. That I do agree with. It's what my father always taught us.

SHELLEY. By fixing men's minds on the idea of an afterlife, they make them wary – terrified even – of all forms of dissent.

MARY. Yes.

SHELLEY. And a crowd of privileged gentlemen called parsons get very well paid to convince their congregations that 'sinning' includes any kind of opposition to governments, or kings or landowners or the waging of wars.

JANE. I hope the vicar isn't listening to this!

MARY. But if you take faith away from people, what do you replace it with? Faith can make people feel stronger. United. And the poor must have more need of it than the rich.

SHELLEY. Because we are human, we have doubts and fears – yes. And we look for something to reassure us.

MARY. And to empower us.

SHELLEY. But imagine how much stronger we could become if we looked only to ourselves and our fellow human beings for the comfort and… philosophy we need.

They have reached the tomb.

Is this it?

MARY. Yes. This is it.

SHELLEY *stares at the tomb. He runs his hands over the stone.*

JANE. Is it how you imagined it would be?

SHELLEY. It's strong. And honest. That seems right.

MARY. This side's usually shady. This is where I sit and read.

JANE. Sometimes I even lie back, like this. (*Lies on top of the tomb.*) But last time I did it, one of the gravediggers came past and stared at me as though I were a lunatic.

SHELLEY (*reading the lettering on the tomb*). 'Mary. Wollstonecraft.'

MARY. My mother believed in God. Her own sense of God.

SHELLEY. Perhaps that's why you want to believe.

MARY. But that's just it – I don't want to believe. I know you're right. Logically. You and my father. But then I look at the world about me, and I think – mankind did not create this. We couldn't create it. And perhaps it is only a form of weakness – arrogance, not to believe in God. Some of the greatest people have turned to God when they are really desperate and afraid. And I can't be entirely sure that I wouldn't.

SHELLEY. But we should never give in to fear.

MARY. Do you not think it would be a comfort – to know that you could one day lie down in a place like this? Safe in the shadow of the church?

SHELLEY. I think I would be happy in some woodland glade. Safe in the shadow of the trees.

Or in a giant mausoleum, on the top of a dusty hill in some Latin land.

JANE. You two are too gloomy! And on such a heavenly day.

SHELLEY. I do believe in the human spirit. Profoundly. I believe we are more than we seem to be.

MARY. Yes.

They are staring at each other – truly connected. JANE *gets up.*

JANE. I'm going to take a turn around the churchyard. All this talk of death is making me want to run about. I suppose neither of you will come?

SHELLEY. I think we might sit here for a while. But call out if you have need of us.

JANE. I shan't be long.

She goes. MARY *and* SHELLEY *are quiet for a few moments.*

MARY. Your poem… *Queen Mab…* When I was reading it…

SHELLEY. What?

MARY. It's so honest. Savagely honest. And so right about the state of the world. And yet you… You seem to contain so much… joy…

SHELLEY. Because I have hope. And belief in what can be achieved. I was fourteen when I first read *Political Justice*. I wept. I suppose it was a sort of relief. To have found that there was someone with the vision and clarity of mind to be able to strip away all that is wrong and useless and present a way of living which would allow mankind to achieve its potential. To achieve perfection. I will never stop striving for that world.

Did you like it – my poem?

MARY. I loved it.

SHELLEY. Do I come close to Byron? Can I?

MARY. I think you are every bit as talented.

He touches her face, momentarily. Then they sit quietly for a moment.

SHELLEY. Thank you for bringing me here.

MARY. It's so peaceful here. Yet we're only a few yards from the streets. The river is just beyond those willows.

Sometimes I come here to write. My thoughts seem to flow more easily when I'm here.

SHELLEY. I like to walk when I'm working, and I always try to memorise – exactly – the lines that come to me. Because I know that when I get back inside, with paper and pen, I will never find the freshness I found in the field or by the stream.

MARY. Yes. Have you started another poem?

SHELLEY. I've tried to. It's been a difficult few days.

MARY. Has it?

SHELLEY. Distracting. Harriet has come. With her sister and the baby. At first it was only to buy a new bonnet – and apparently there are only a handful of London shops that are good enough for bonnets – but now it seems she has decided to stay longer. And she says my lodgings aren't suitable, so I've been running around trying to find somewhere better.

MARY. That is difficult.

SHELLEY. Yes. Not that I'm complaining. It's only that… these domestic things… they seem so trivial sometimes. And…

MARY. I love you.

He stops. Their hearts leap.

SHELLEY. When I get the money I'm expecting, perhaps I will buy a house. Close to here…

He kisses her – suddenly and passionately.

Oh, Mary. Mary. I love you. I love you. From the very first moment I saw you. Can it be true? Oh, no – no – don't cry.

MARY. I can't help it.

SHELLEY. Beautiful. You are so beautiful.

They kiss.

MARY. What are we going to do?

SHELLEY. I…

He can't answer. After a moment, they hear JANE approaching. MARY dries her eyes.

JANE. Two rabbits and a jay. Such a dandy in his pink and blue.

Ah. You know it's completely obvious.

MARY. What is?

JANE. I'm not such a fool as all that.

SHELLEY. Jane…

JANE. I know. I know. And it's utterly, unspeakably thrilling.

Scene Two

The parlour. Skinner Street. MARY and JANE enter. JANE rushes straight to the window. Voices can be heard coming from behind the closed door of the study. JANE suddenly waves enthusiastically.

JANE. He turned back to look. You should have waved.

   MARY *is too overwhelmed with her excitement to respond.*

   Oh, Mary.

   What did he say? I want to know everything.

MARY. It was I who spoke first.

JANE. You?

MARY. But he had already touched my face.

JANE. He touched your face? And did he… I mean, did he kiss you?

MARY. Yes.

JANE. Oh!

MARY. Yes, he did. We mustn't say anything to Papa.

JANE. No! Or to Mama.

MARY. But will you help me? Help me to meet him again?

JANE. Of course I will. Mary, I must confess, I am the tiniest bit jealous, but you will allow me that, I think?

MARY. Oh, Jane.

JANE. And deep down, I think I always knew. I always knew that he would choose you, because you are her real daughter, and Papa is your real papa. He was bound to be drawn to you.

FANNY *enters from the study. We hear the voices of* GODWIN *and* MRS GODWIN, *rather heated.*

FANNY. Secrets?

MARY. No.

JANE. No. We were just talking.

FANNY. Where have you been?

MARY. We just went for a walk. To the churchyard.

FANNY. Well, I wish you hadn't been so long.

JANE. Are they arguing?

FANNY. I had to close the shop for an hour. I don't know why you two think you can go off to the churchyard whenever you like and just leave me to...

JANE. We had promised Mr Shelley.

FANNY. You took Shelley?

MARY. Yes. To show him Mother's grave. We said we would. Remember?

FANNY. I wish you'd asked me. I would have liked to have come. Very much.

MARY. I'm sorry. I assumed you were busy.

JANE. What are they arguing about?

FANNY. Me. About whether I should go and spend some days with my aunts. They're in Wales. By the sea. Mama thinks she cannot spare me. Judging by today, I would say she's right.

JANE. Oh, don't be so hoity-toity, Fanny.

FANNY *decides to try to let the matter rest*.

FANNY. How was Shelley?

MARY. Well. Do you want to go to the seaside?

FANNY. Yes. I do. Papa thinks my aunts are going to ask me to go and work at the school in Dublin.

JANE. Really?

MARY. Would you?

FANNY. I think so. I think it would be good for me to have some new society. And proper employment. A little income of my own.

MARY. Yes.

FANNY. If I stay here always… Well… I don't suppose anything will ever happen.

MRS GODWIN *enters, shortly followed by* GODWIN.

MRS GODWIN. One day you shall find that I am not here, Mr Godwin. I shall take myself off to the seaside.

GODWIN. We shall very soon have the maid back…

MRS GODWIN. No other woman in her right mind would put up with what I am expected to put up with.

GODWIN. I know. We are all very fortunate to have you.

MRS GODWIN. This is not what I was promised!

(*Starts to go then turns on* FANNY.) I hope you're satisfied! Ungrateful girl!

It will kill me. That's all. Kill me.

She rushes out.

FANNY. Papa, if it's going to cause such a deal of trouble…

GODWIN. You may write to your aunts and tell them you will accept their kind invitation.

FANNY. Very well. Thank you.

GODWIN. Go after your mother, if you please, Jane. Do something. Tea, perhaps.

JANE. Yes, Papa.

She goes.

MARY. Are you all right, Papa?

GODWIN. Yes. Weathered worse.

He goes back to his study.

MARY. What a performance. She acts as though she never has a holiday. Didn't she go to Kent last summer?

FANNY. I suppose that seems a long time ago now. She does work hard.

MARY. Yes, but...

FANNY. And there was an incident at lunchtime which upset her. One of Papa's creditors came to the door. Mama saw him. He was very rude. Threatening almost.

MARY. Do we owe a lot of people money?

FANNY. It will all be all right soon. The business with Shelley's bond is almost done. Mary, I don't think you and Jane should have walked out with Mr Shelley.

MARY. We didn't walk out with him. We took him to see Mother's grave.

FANNY. Seeing him here is one thing, but to be seen about the streets with him...

MARY. You said you wanted to come.

FANNY. ...without Mama or Papa, or his wife. I don't think you should do that.

MARY. How very conventional.

FANNY. All I am saying, is that we should all, all of us, tread a little carefully. He is a married man.

MARY *scoffs.*

It means something, Mary.

MARY. Surely it would be worse if he wasn't married?

FANNY. We have to respect the fact that he is not at liberty to... he is not at liberty.

> MARY *looks down*. FANNY *is silent for a moment*.

Has something happened?

MARY. No.

FANNY. If you think of walking out with him again, please tell Papa.

MARY. You sound terribly old when you talk like that, Fanny.

FANNY. Don't do that.

> I must get on.

> *She starts to go*.

MARY. Fanny, I'm sorry.

> FANNY *comes back to her and kisses her hand*.

> I'm sorry. Our mother loved a married man. Before she even met your father.

FANNY. Yes. And she realised that nothing would come of it. Nothing except heartache, and loss.

> Loving... may be beautiful, but it's complicated. Always complicated. I know that much.

> *She leaves*.

Scene Three

Evening. St Pancras Churchyard. SHELLEY *is waiting by Mary Wollstonecraft's tomb.* MARY *and* JANE *appear and rush towards him. They all embrace, and then* SHELLEY *kisses* MARY *passionately.*

JANE. Go. Go. I'll keep watch.

> MARY *and* SHELLEY *move into the shelter of the tomb, and fall into each other's arms. Their embraces become*

increasingly daring and sexual, until SHELLEY *stops for a moment, and takes hold of* MARY*'s face, staring into her eyes.*

SHELLEY. I am yours now. Only yours. Even though I must go back to her…

MARY. Don't.

SHELLEY.… you must lie down tonight and know that I am with you. My heart conjoined with yours. My soul within your body.

MARY. I cannot live without you.

SHELLEY. You will not have to. We will be together. Soon. There will be no lies. No pretence. This is the truth now.

They fall into embraces once again.

Scene Four

Evening. The parlour. Skinner Street. GODWIN, MRS GODWIN, MARY, JANE *and* SHELLEY *are sitting together.*

MRS GODWIN *is pouring wine.*

GODWIN. To the very top, Mrs Godwin. To the very top.

MRS GODWIN. That is the top! It's almost overflowing!

GODWIN. I think we need a bacchanalian flavour to our revelries tonight. What do you say, Shelley?

SHELLEY. Certainly. Let us shame the gods.

GODWIN. I'm only sorry that Fanny is not with us. She worked as hard as anyone towards this day.

JANE. We must write to her in Wales.

GODWIN. Indeed we must. (*To* MRS GODWIN.) That's it. That's it. Mary too.

MARY. Just a little more then.

MRS GODWIN. You will have us all inebriated.

GODWIN. And a song, Jane. Will you oblige us with a song?

SHELLEY. A song!

JANE. What shall I sing?

MRS GODWIN. She sings beautifully, Mr Shelley.

SHELLEY. Does she?

MRS GODWIN. We paid for lessons. Sing the one you were
    practising, Jane.

JANE. But I don't know that one properly yet.

GODWIN. Any song. Any song. I shall sing myself in a minute
    and then where will we be?

JANE. Oh, I know!

She begins to sing a pretty, happy song.

SHELLEY. Ah, yes. I've heard this one.

JANE (*faltering*). Oh, no… I can't remember the last bit…

    MARY *joins in to help her, quickly followed by* SHELLEY
    and the GODWINS. *They finish the song.*

MRS GODWIN. Well, that is jolly.

GODWIN. Bravo, Jane!

SHELLEY. You do sing beautifully.

JANE. Do I? Oh, thank you.

GODWIN. Now, I think a few words are in order.

MRS GODWIN. Oh yes, I should say so. Order! Order!

JANE. Oh, Maman!

GODWIN. Yes. As you know, Shelley, I set very little store by
    gratitude. But what I offer you this evening, is my respect.
    My heartfelt respect. There are many men who claim to
    believe in the revolution which is *Political Justice*, but few
    who are prepared to put it at the very centre of the way they
    live their lives. Today, with the arrival of the pecuniary

cavalry, shall we say, I think we have struck a small blow against the forces of reaction. Against the criminality of property rights, of inheritance, and of the land-owning class. A blow which I vow to capitalise on, to the very best of my ability, with every moment of my labour. We are liberators! Liberators, no less, of the resources of mankind!

SHELLEY. Hear! Hear!

GODWIN (*raising his glass*). To *Political Justice*!

ALL. *Political Justice!*

They all drink.

MRS GODWIN. What a day! What a day for us all.

GODWIN. More wine required, Mrs Godwin.

MRS GODWIN. More wine? Good heavens above, Mr Godwin!

GODWIN. Shelley's glass is empty, look.

SHELLEY. But I've had plenty. It doesn't take very much to...

GODWIN. Can't have that. Two bottles, my dearest. In the kitchen. If you would?

MRS GODWIN *leaves.*

JANE. It's so delicious, isn't it, Mary?

MARY. Yes.

SHELLEY. I have no wish for gratitude, Godwin. I hope you know that. And I think you know what your respect means to me.

GODWIN. Yes, my friend. I believe I do.

Pause.

SHELLEY. I wonder if you would care for a stroll?

GODWIN. A stroll? Now?

SHELLEY. Yes. It is such a balmy evening. And I would welcome the opportunity to discuss certain things with you.

MARY. It is a lovely evening, Papa.

GODWIN. I don't think my legs would get me down the stairs tonight. No, no. Let us stay here. A Skinner Street celebration. High spirits at Skinner Street, eh?

So, the money has arrived with your bankers?

SHELLEY. Yes. They assured me I will be able to give you your share tomorrow.

GODWIN. In cash?

SHELLEY. If that's what you would like?

GODWIN. Yes, I think that would be best. No names involved. And easier to distribute, of course.

SHELLEY. But, Godwin, I must warn you... the amount... your share, will be a little less than we discussed.

GODWIN. What's that?

JANE. I will go and help Mama.

MARY. Yes.

SHELLEY. I have decided we must split the money down the middle. One thousand, two hundred and fifty each, to be precise. The fact is, I have need of more money than I realised.

GODWIN. But I have need of the amount we agreed upon. Two thousand, Shelley. One thousand... it is enough to cover my most pressing debts, but beyond that...

SHELLEY. We can sell another bond. Soon, if you wish.

The fact is, Godwin, Mary and I are entirely in love. And we mean to be together. We plan to go abroad. We think that would make things easier for everyone. And we both have the desire to travel.

GODWIN. What are you talking about?

MARY. We love each other, Papa.

SHELLEY. We plan to go to the Continent. We shall travel down through France. I have told Harriet. Of course, I must continue to provide for her... so I will need a great deal more money than I anticipated.

GODWIN. No...

MRS GODWIN *enters with the wine*.

MRS GODWIN. Now, who's for a little more?

GODWIN. Out. Please. Please leave us for a moment.

MRS GODWIN. Whatever's the matter?

GODWIN. Leave us. Please.

MRS GODWIN *leaves, reluctantly. There is a silence*.

MARY. I'm sorry if we've shocked you, Papa. But we thought you would rather know the truth.

GODWIN. I will not allow this.

MARY. But…

SHELLEY. We are decided. We are inseparable. Our love is a fact which must be acted upon.

Pause.

GODWIN. I would like to speak to Mr Shelley alone, Mary.

MARY. But I would rather… No… I would rather hear what you have to say.

GODWIN. I will speak to him alone. Kindly go to your room.

MARY. But…

SHELLEY (*to* MARY). It's all right. It's all right. Don't worry.

She leaves.

It is a cause to rejoice, Godwin. I'm sure that you will come to see that.

GODWIN. I hardly know where to begin.

SHELLEY. It took us by surprise. It has been overwhelming. A revelation.

GODWIN. If you cannot see that everything about this proposal is wrong… in every possible sense…

SHELLEY. But why?

GODWIN. Why? Have you forgotten that you are a married man? That you have a wife and a child, and another on the way, from all accounts?

SHELLEY. My marriage is over. For my part, at least. And as you say in *Political Justice*, a marriage should not be made to continue if one of the partners decides it is no longer what...

GODWIN. And if you read the second edition of *Political Justice*, you would see that I put forward a very different opinion on what marriage must mean in...

SHELLEY. Oh, I never read second editions. You know that. Second editions are the fruits of fear. First editions with the guts ripped out.

GODWIN. You are quite wrong. Second editions allow time for reflection...

SHELLEY. You mean for qualification?

GODWIN. Ideas should always be allowed to evolve. It is imperative that they evolve. And I did not ever mean to suggest that any relationship between two people should attempt to exist outside the mores of society in its present state...

SHELLEY. I believe in what you originally wrote, Godwin. Even if you do not. And the more I live, the more I know that you were right.

GODWIN. I was speaking of an ideal world, Shelley.

SHELLEY. Then let us begin it now. For if we do not, who will? I will not be enslaved by the expectations of society. And neither will Mary.

GODWIN. Please do not assume to speak for my daughter. I know my daughter a great deal better than you.

GODWIN *fights to recover his composure.*

SHELLEY. I'm sorry if we have upset you...

GODWIN. I cannot give my permission for what you propose.

I would like you to go now, Shelley. I will come and see you tomorrow afternoon about the money – if that would be acceptable?

SHELLEY. Certainly.

GODWIN. We will talk further then. I would like you to think about what I have said.

SHELLEY. It will make no difference.

GODWIN. And in the meantime, I must ask that you do not attempt to see Mary.

SHELLEY. Before tomorrow afternoon?

GODWIN. Yes. In the first instance. If you would oblige me in that?

SHELLEY. Very well. But I must say goodbye to her now.

GODWIN. No. I will say goodbye on your behalf. I think that best. I will see you tomorrow.

SHELLEY. It will make no difference.

SHELLEY *leaves*. GODWIN *stands very still, trying to process the shock. After a few moments*, MRS GODWIN *enters*. JANE *hovers behind her in the doorway*.

MRS GODWIN. Are you going to tell me what is going on?

MARY *rushes in*.

MARY. Has he gone?

GODWIN. Yes.

MARY. What did you say to him?

When is he coming back? Papa?

MRS GODWIN. Oh, I see. I see now, what it is.

I might have guessed. I suppose I should just be thankful that it isn't Jane.

(*To* MARY.) Has he touched you? Has he?

MARY. Oh, don't be so vulgar.

MRS GODWIN. You… I should flay the hide off you!

GODWIN. No! We will be civilised.

MRS GODWIN (*to* JANE). Did you know about this?

JANE. I…

GODWIN. He says goodbye to you, Mary. Now let us all get some rest.

MARY. What did you say to him?

GODWIN. I said what any father would say: that you are a sixteen-year-old girl, and that he is a married man.

MARY. I can't believe you're behaving like this. You're behaving like the worst kind of autocrat. Forgive me, but you are. Would you really have preferred it if we were to sneak around behind your back? Lying? Pretending that things are other than they are?

MRS GODWIN. He would have preferred it if you hadn't gone near each other in the first place! Have you any idea what this will do to us? To our reputation?

MARY. I don't care about any of that!

MRS GODWIN. Well, you should! And then there is the money. What is going to happen with…

GODWIN. We shall have the money. Now… that is enough. Enough. I will not hear another word on the subject. Not tonight. Let us put an end to this day. To bed. Everyone.

MARY *does not move.*

Go to bed, Mary.

MARY. And we will talk tomorrow?

GODWIN. Yes.

She goes. JANE *follows her.*

MRS GODWIN. I tried to warn you. But did you listen?

As you sow, so shall you reap.

GODWIN *leaves suddenly.*

Scene Five

Early afternoon. Two days later. The parlour. Skinner Street.
MRS GODWIN *is setting the table for tea.* JANE *rushes in. She
is wearing her outdoor shawl.*

JANE. Mary? Oh.

MRS GODWIN. Where have you been?

JANE. I went to get bread. You said we needed some.

MRS GODWIN. Where is it, then?

JANE. I put it in the kitchen. Really, Maman.

MRS GODWIN. Tell me next time you think of leaving this
  house. Do you understand?

JANE. I was only gone a few minutes. I was only trying to help.

  What's going on? The best china. Is someone coming?

  MRS GODWIN *glances out of the window.*

MRS GODWIN. They're here.

JANE. Who are?

MRS GODWIN. Go and fetch madam from the bedroom. Tell
  her to come here at once. And then you can stay too. I want
  you to hear this.

JANE. Who is it?

MRS GODWIN. Do as I say.

  JANE *hurries out.* MRS GODWIN *puts the finishing touches
  to the table, and straightens her skirts. After a moment,*
  GODWIN *escorts* HARRIET SHELLEY *into the room.*
  HARRIET *is about six months pregnant.*

GODWIN. Please come in. You remember Mrs Godwin?

MRS GODWIN. Of course she does. I'm sorry we meet again under such trying circumstances. It is very upsetting for us all, I'm sure. Would you care for some tea?

HARRIET. No, thank you. I do not wish to stay any longer than I must.

JANE *appears in the doorway and stops*.

GODWIN. Jane.

JANE *enters*.

Jane is our youngest daughter.

MRS GODWIN. My daughter.

MARY *enters*.

GODWIN. And this is Mary.

Mary, I would like you to meet Mrs Shelley.

JANE *gasps slightly*.

Perhaps we had better sit down.

MARY *and* HARRIET *remain standing*.

MARY. Papa…?

GODWIN. Mrs Shelley has been made acquainted with her husband's situation regarding you, Mary. Quite naturally, she has certain things she wishes to say to you.

MARY. I cannot think that this… can be of any benefit to any of us.

HARRIET. My husband is very erratic, Miss Godwin. He becomes extremely impassioned, dedicated to something, and then he just as quickly loses interest in it. He drops it.

It is simply his nature. I am sorry for it.

His love for me… was intense. And though I accept that the nature of his love has changed somewhat of late, it is still love. He loves me. As a husband loves a wife. That is apparent, I think.

We have a daughter. Did you know? Ianthe. After the maiden in his poem. The poem he dedicated to me. She is not yet two. This baby will be born in September. I think it will be a boy. We hope it will be. I see you are not without feeling. I would like to think there is not a woman on earth who would willingly deprive a child of its father. Even animals, I believe, stay close to their young in order to protect them.

She is becoming distressed.

GODWIN. Please do sit down.

MRS GODWIN (*offering a chair*). Here.

HARRIET *sits*.

HARRIET. I have been in this situation before. Hardly six months ago. He became rather too close to the wife of one of his friends. I will not name the lady. But I have made Mr Godwin aware of the details – in case he should have need of them. They do not see each other now. Her husband took her away. But you see, you are not the first.

Please don't imagine that you are.

GODWIN. Mary, Mrs Shelley and I would like you to give us your word that you will have no further contact with Shelley.

MARY *sways slightly, as though her legs will give way.*

JANE. Ah!

MRS GODWIN. Leave her.

GODWIN. You can now be under no illusion as to the damage this situation could engender. Let it stop now.

Do we have your word?

Mary?

MARY (*almost inaudibly*). Yes.

GODWIN. Good. Later, I shall ask you to put it in writing. But for now, that will suffice.

HARRIET (*to* GODWIN). Thank you.

She stands to go.

(*To* MARY.) Do you believe in God?

He is your witness. As well as I.

MRS GODWIN. Shall I show you out, my dear?

HARRIET. Good day.

She leaves with MRS GODWIN. *In the silence,* JANE *sobs suddenly.* GODWIN *looks at* MARY.

GODWIN. It needed doing. For your sake as much as anyone's. It is over, Mary. I saw Shelley earlier today, and said the same thing to him.

MARY. May I go now?

GODWIN. I have written to Fanny and asked her to come home immediately.

MARY. May I go now?

GODWIN. You are young. You will soon recover. You don't need him, Mary.

MARY *leaves*.

Scene Six

The bedroom. The beds and floor are littered with Mary Wollstonecraft's books. MARY *enters. She is distressed and angry and frightened – overwhelmed with conflicting emotions. She collapses to her knees.*

She takes up one of the books and clutches it to her heart.

JANE *enters, cautiously.*

JANE. That was so cruel. I'm so sorry.

MARY *turns away from her touch.*

MARY. Don't. Please.

JANE *takes a scrap of paper from her pocket, and gives it to* MARY.

JANE. Here. It's from him.

MARY. You saw him?

JANE. He sent someone into the shop. I went to meet him. He is desperate. Quite desperate.

MARY reads the note.

He wants you to go away with him, doesn't he? To elope.

MARY. Yes.

JANE. Mary, if you want to go, I will come with you. He thinks I should. I could be so useful to you. I can speak French. Think what a help that would be. And I cannot stay here. Mama is already treating me like a prisoner. Imagine what it will be like after you've gone.

MARY. She has his child. She loves him.

JANE. But he does not love her. She isn't right for him. It was a mistake.

MARY. Would you please leave me, Jane?

JANE. Oh, my poor Mary. You will answer him, won't you? He's waiting for your answer. I will find a way to take it to him.

MARY. Thank you.

JANE starts to go, then pauses.

JANE. There is no life but loving.

JANE leaves.

In her mind, MARY sees HARRIET struggling in the river, just as her mother did. HARRIET is trying to hold the baby's head above the water, even as she forces her own head under.

MARY can bear it no longer. She closes her eyes and covers her ears, and buries her face.

Scene Seven

Night. The bedroom. MARY *and* JANE *are asleep. Raised voices can be heard downstairs, and a little screech of alarm.* MARY *awakens and sits up. She listens.*

MARY. Jane. Jane. Wake up.

> JANE *wakes up, slowly.*

I think he's here.

JANE. Shelley?

MARY. I heard his voice. It's him. I know it is.

> MARY *is on her feet.* MRS GODWIN *enters. She is in her dressing gown.*

MRS GODWIN. Back into bed.

MARY. Is it Shelley? What's happening?

MRS GODWIN. Yes, it is Shelley. And I never saw a man in such a state. He's taken something – that's obvious.

JANE. What do you mean?

MRS GODWIN. Laudanum or something of the sort.

JANE. Oh, no!

MARY. I want to see him.

MRS GODWIN. His eyes are as wide as saucers. Mr Godwin is going to walk him about the streets. And try to talk some sense into him. Your poor father. At this time of night.

MARY. I can walk him round the streets. Papa doesn't have to.

MRS GODWIN. And this is the sort of man you want to throw away your life for? None of them are worth it. Let me tell you. For all their promises and their grand gestures. They're weak. Weak inside. And they leave us to pay the price for it.

MARY. You don't know him at all!

Downstairs, a door is heard closing. MARY *rushes to the window and starts to open it.* MRS GODWIN *rushes forward and pushes her aside, roughly and desperately.*

JANE. Mary!

MRS GODWIN (*distressed*). Now look what you've done. Please. Just settle down. This place has become a madhouse, and I shan't have it.

She leaves. MARY *is trembling.*

JANE. Do you think he'll be all right?

It's frightening. Laudanum.

MARY. Find me a pen, will you?

JANE. A pen?

JANE *finds one, and* MARY *takes up a piece of paper.* MARY *takes the pen, and begins to write.*

Is it your answer?

MARY. Yes.

Scene Eight

Early morning. Two days later. GODWIN'*s study.* GODWIN *enters and opens the curtains. He goes to his desk, preparing to start work. He notices a note on the top of some books. He looks at it for a moment, before picking it up and reading it.*

MRS GODWIN *rushes in.*

MRS GODWIN. Where are the girls? They're not in their...

GODWIN. They've gone.

With him.

MRS GODWIN. Gone?

GODWIN. To France, I assume. Apparently they will write as soon as they arrive at their destination.

MRS GODWIN. But… But not Jane? Why? Why would she…? Oh, no. Oh, no. Jane.

GODWIN. Who would have thought they could be so quiet?

MRS GODWIN. We must get the first coach to Dover. They can't have been gone very long. We shall have to close the shop. Well, it can't be helped. If we stop them quickly, no one…

GODWIN. I will not go after them.

MRS GODWIN. Yes you will. Of course you will.

GODWIN. I will not. She gave me her word.

MRS GODWIN. Then I will!

She rushes out. GODWIN *is white-faced with anger and shock. He reads the note again, then crumples it in his hand.*

In another part of the stage, we see FANNY, *in Wales, opening* GODWIN's *letter containing the news about* MARY *and* SHELLEY. *She feels as though she has been dealt a physical blow.*

FANNY. Oh, no. Mary. Mary.

It grows dark. In a boat, on the Channel, MARY, SHELLEY *and* JANE *are being rowed across to France. It is cold, and the water beneath them is black and churning.* MARY *is lying with her head against* SHELLEY's *chest. She is thinking of her father and of* FANNY. *But a kiss from* SHELLEY *is enough to recall her to the relief and pleasure of being with him.*

The boat moves on, over the water.

End of Act Two.

ACT THREE

Scene One

MARY is dreaming. In her dream, it is night. She is on a mountain top. The wind is howling. Thunder crashes overhead. Ahead of her is a figure dressed in black. She clambers towards it, stumbling. She calls out in desperation.

MARY. Father!

The figure turns and stares at her with hostility. It is GODWIN. Then he turns away from her and walks on.

Scene Two

Night. A lofty room, in a large dilapidated house in Switzerland. MARY is trying to open the shutters at the window, as quietly as she can. SHELLEY and JANE are sleeping on a bed. SHELLEY awakens and comes to her.

SHELLEY. Mary?

MARY. I woke up. I can't get back to sleep.

SHELLEY. You're not feeling unwell again?

MARY. No. I didn't mean to disturb you.

He puts his arms around her and kisses her.

I was hoping a little light might come in, but there isn't any moon tonight. I was going to write in the journal.

SHELLEY. Good idea.

MARY. That's the last of the candle.

SHELLEY. I know.

MARY. We'll have to get some more tomorrow.

SHELLEY. Yes.

MARY. Where will we get them from?

SHELLEY. I don't know. We'll have to walk down to the village and knock on people's doors. What's the French for candle?

MARY. They won't even open their doors. It's as though they're afraid of us.

Shelley, I don't like this house. I know the mountains are wonderful – and the skies, and the air. But there's something melancholy about this place.

SHELLEY. Something hostile.

MARY. Yes. I wish we hadn't taken it. Six months. Right through the winter.

SHELLEY. I tried to light the stove after you came up to bed. It doesn't work.

MARY. What?

SHELLEY. No wonder the owners were smiling when they handed over the keys.

MARY. Do we have any money left? Please tell me – I'd rather know.

SHELLEY. Not much. About twenty pounds. Just enough to get home with.

MARY. Is that what you want to do?

SHELLEY. I don't know what else we can do. My watch was the last valuable thing I had. No one's going to send us any money from England. I've left a trail of debts.

MARY. I dreamt about my father again just now.

SHELLEY. What did you dream?

MARY. Do you remember that desolate village we passed through – the one where the Cossacks had been through and taken everything?

SHELLEY. Yes.

MARY. I dreamt I was there. Alone – I mean, without you and Jane. It was night. I saw a figure emerging from between two of the houses. Moving silently. Dressed in black. And I followed him, and when I got closer, I could see that it was my father. He moved through the village, up towards the hills. I could hardly keep up, he was moving so fast. And I knew that he was making for the tower that we saw – the dark tower on the headland.

SHELLEY. Yes. I remember it.

MARY. And I wanted to stop him before he got there. I had to. And I called out to him, but the wind blew the words back into my mouth. Then he stopped suddenly, and he looked round at me. And his look was so cold. So forbidding. And he turned away. And then I woke up.

SHELLEY. You have to write that down.

MARY. When I think of him, I have this feeling of dismay, deep inside. I've disappointed him.

SHELLEY. He was shocked, that's all. He'll come to see the situation more reasonably. He probably already has. It must be hard, I know. You've been close to him.

MARY. Yes.

SHELLEY. My parents were always so distant from me. But I'm glad, in a way. Those family ties; they're not entirely useful. They can stop us from pursuing what's really important. Would your father – or your mother – ever have written anything if they'd stayed in their villages? Stayed with their families?

MARY. Probably not.

SHELLEY. We cannot put the needs of our loved ones before the greater good. We cannot be ruled by sentimentality.

MARY. *Political Justice*.

SHELLEY. Yes. It's pure *Political Justice*. We'll re-read those chapters tomorrow. It will help.

MARY. Thank you.

I see Jane's with us again.

SHELLEY. She heard rats in her room. I couldn't turn her away. You don't mind, do you?

MARY. I suppose I wouldn't want to sleep alone in this house.

Let's write in the journal.

SHELLEY. Yes.

MARY *places the journal next to the candle and takes up a pen.*

MARY. I'll write something, and then you can write.

SHELLEY. One day people will read this journal, and they'll know that we were really living.

Scene Three

The parlour. Skinner Street. GODWIN *is sorting through a pile of books.* MRS GODWIN *is working on an inventory.* FANNY *enters carrying a small parcel of books.*

FANNY. I've found a few more copies of *Lessons for Children.*

GODWIN. Ah. Where were they?

FANNY. In the spare room. Under some blankets. There are… five.

GODWIN. Very good. Add them to the inventory, Mrs Godwin.

MRS GODWIN. A fat lot of difference that will make.

FANNY. When is the valuer coming about the copyrights, Papa?

GODWIN. Tomorrow, I hope. If he can fit us in.

FANNY. Did he give any indication of what they might be worth?

GODWIN. No. But he's a good man. Thorough. He'll make sure we don't undersell ourselves.

MRS GODWIN. Undersell ourselves to whom? Mr Nobody? Nobody is going to buy this business. Nobody would be mad enough.

GODWIN. I disagree.

MRS GODWIN. And we certainly won't find a buyer in time.

GODWIN. It's a promising concern for anyone with some capital to invest.

MRS GODWIN. It's a disaster. It has been from the very start. When I think of the hours I've spent, running to and fro to the printers, standing behind that counter in the draughts, writing into the small hours. And where has it got us?

FANNY. It hasn't been a complete disaster, Mama. We've just been a little unlucky with investment and…

MRS GODWIN. Oh, you don't know anything about it. Don't pretend you do. I feel sick.

FANNY. Please don't upset yourself.

MRS GODWIN. I really think I'm going to be sick.

GODWIN. Then please do it quietly. These figures won't add themselves.

MRS GODWIN. And Charles won't even come home to help. I am abandoned by my own son.

There is a knock on the door of the shop downstairs. They all stop dead.

Oh, my good Lord.

FANNY. Are we expecting anyone?

MRS GODWIN. What if it's the bailiffs?

GODWIN. How could it possibly be? We haven't yet heard from the court.

The banging comes again. FANNY *goes to the window and looks out, cautiously.*

MRS GODWIN. Don't be seen, you silly girl!

FANNY. Shall I go down, Papa?

GODWIN. Yes. But check who it is before you open the door.

FANNY. I will.

She leaves.

MRS GODWIN. What if it's the bailiffs?

GODWIN. Try to control yourself, my dear. I'm quite sure it won't be.

MRS GODWIN. I can't go to prison, Mr Godwin.

GODWIN. I know. I doubt very much that it will come to that.

MRS GODWIN. Would it help if I went to see this monstrous man who wants to ruin us?

GODWIN. I don't think that would help.

MRS GODWIN. I can be very charming when I need to be.

GODWIN. It's not personal. He has no wish to see us destitute. He simply wants his money. And he no longer cares how he gets it. If we should find ourselves in prison…

MRS GODWIN. Oh, don't…

GODWIN.…my friends and my supporters will rally round, I'm sure, and…

MRS GODWIN. And what can they do? None of them has the sort of money we need. A bunch of useless old wastrels.

FANNY *enters. She has a note in her hand.*

FANNY. It's a letter. I think it's from him.

MRS GODWIN. From the creditor?

FANNY. No. I think it's from Shelley. It's his handwriting.

She hands the letter to GODWIN, *who opens it.*

MRS GODWIN. Shelley? What does it say?

GODWIN. Hardly a letter. He thinks this a fit way to communicate.

MRS GODWIN. What does he say? Where was it posted?

GODWIN. They're back.

FANNY. Back? In England?

GODWIN. Yes.

MRS GODWIN. Oh, thank God.

FANNY. Are they safe? Well?

GODWIN. It would seem so. They've taken lodgings.

MRS GODWIN. You mean, they're not coming here?

FANNY. Whereabouts?

GODWIN. St Marylebone.

MRS GODWIN. That's miles away!

FANNY. It's not so far.

MRS GODWIN (*to* GODWIN). You said they would come back here. You said they would come back with their tails between their legs.

GODWIN *does not reply.*

Well. I suppose I had better get dressed, if I'm going all the way to Marylebone.

GODWIN. Nobody will be going to see them.

MRS GODWIN. But…

GODWIN. Nor will they be admitted to this house. Not unless they apologise and ask to return on a permanent basis.

MRS GODWIN. But I want to see Jane. I haven't seen her for months. I can only imagine what a state she's in. What if he is keeping her against her will?

GODWIN. I think Jane made it clear to you in Dover that it is very much her will to remain with Mr Shelley. I will not have you humiliating yourself by going after her again.

MRS GODWIN. But she might have changed her mind.

GODWIN. This says she has not.

Pause.

FANNY. I could go. I could take them any message you wish to send.

GODWIN. No one shall go. Now let us get on with our task. We have more important matters to deal with.

Scene Four

Day. Outside a tavern. A noisy street. FANNY is waiting. SHELLEY arrives and rushes to her.

SHELLEY. Fanny! I wasn't sure that you would come.

Hello.

FANNY. Hello.

SHELLEY. You found it all right. Hardly the most salubrious place to meet.

FANNY. I can't stay long. If he knew where I was…

SHELLEY. How could he know? Unless he's taken to following you? Has he?

FANNY. No. But it took me an hour to walk here. He'll be wondering where I've gone. And if he asks me… you know I can't lie to him.

SHELLEY. It's his fault we have to meet like this. You know we came to the shop two days ago? We stood on the street for almost half an hour.

FANNY. Yes.

SHELLEY. Were you in?

FANNY. We were all in.

How's Mary? How's Jane?

SHELLEY. They're well. Thriving. Mary's pregnant.

FANNY. Oh.

SHELLEY. It took us an age to realise it. But it's quite obvious now.

FANNY. I see.

SHELLEY. We're overjoyed. Although I don't know quite how we will manage. Things are rather difficult – financially. In fact I've been running around all morning trying to find a friend who can lend me enough for the rent. The landlady is getting belligerent.

FANNY. I'm sorry. It's dreadful – being in debt. Crushing.

SHELLEY. Are things bad at Skinner Street?

FANNY. They've never been worse.

SHELLEY *looks down in shame.*

It's not your fault.

SHELLEY. I wish I could have given him more, but…

FANNY. It's not your fault.

Will you tell Jane that I'm sure her mother would see her, if she came to the house alone. If she waited until my father went out.

SHELLEY. Yes.

FANNY. Mama is quite unwell. She's desperate to see Jane.

SHELLEY. I'll tell her. Will you tell Godwin about the baby for us?

FANNY. I can't. He has forbidden me from having any contact with you. He checks the post.

SHELLEY. Of course.

FANNY. Write to him.

SHELLEY. You think we should? We didn't want to put it in a letter.

FANNY. You must. It might make a difference. I hope it will.

Pause.

SHELLEY. This is how it's to be then, Fanny. Two camps. Enemy lines. And you're the only one who can cross them. If anyone can bring us all together again, it's you.

FANNY. I don't know why you think that.

SHELLEY. I have faith in you. I always have had.

FANNY. Why?

MARY enters, and approaches cautiously.

MARY. Hello, Fanny.

FANNY looks astonished. Her face flushes.

FANNY. Mary. Mary. I'm glad… about your baby. I have to go.

MARY. But don't.

FANNY. I'm sorry. I didn't know that you would be here. I promised him.

She rushes away.

MARY. Fanny!

FANNY has gone.

How absurd. How ridiculous.

SHELLEY. Don't be too hard on her. We…

MARY. What does she think he can do to her? She's a grown woman. How stupid…

SHELLEY. Mary…

MARY. How stupid.

MARY walks off. SHELLEY goes after her.

Scene Five

Day. The parlour. Skinner Street. JANE *is sitting with* MRS GODWIN *and* FANNY.

JANE. I think we must have looked rather funny – trekking through France on an ass. And it wasn't even a very good ass. It couldn't even carry two of us. In fact there were times when we had to carry *it*. But we did see some wonderful places.

You really ought to try travelling, Fanny. I feel quite different now. Quite changed. We took a large house in a village. It was terribly dark and gloomy. Shelley and I were sure that it was haunted. And it was cold – even in August! But then the stove broke and we had to leave. I thought that was a little rash – just because the stove needed mending. Actually, I've started to think it might have had something to do with money. We certainly aren't living as I supposed a baronet would live.

MRS GODWIN. He's not a baronet. Not yet.

JANE. But then, he is so far above all things material.

MRS GODWIN. And I dare say he never will be if he carries on like this.

JANE. I must say, Fanny, France was a great deal dirtier than I'd imagined it would be.

FANNY. Oh. I suppose it's still recovering from the war…

JANE. And rough does not begin to describe some of the people we were forced to mix with. Why, one night, we were going up the stairs to bed in this horrible, filthy *pension*, when the landlord stopped us and asked if he could join us! Can you imagine. He caught hold of my skirt. He said three wasn't a good number, and he thought I would be left out. I assured him I wouldn't be, but we had to bar the door for the whole night, just in case. And then on the way home, we travelled on a boat up the Rhine and the sailors – well, even Shelley found it hard to be civil.

MRS GODWIN. You slept in the same room?

JANE. Of course. Lots of times. Oh, don't look like that, Mama. You really are terribly 'worldly'. It's hard to define the connection the three of us have. Shelley is passionate about the idea of 'community'. He could never be happy living with just one person. That's what we want to start – a community. He wants to bring his sisters to join us in Marylebone.

FANNY. His sisters? Surely they wouldn't be allowed to…

JANE. He wants to rescue them. Like he rescued us. And he asked Harriet to come too. He wrote her such sweet letters, but she says she won't come. You heard she had the baby? Shelley's simply delighted about it. He's been grinning from ear to ear. A son and heir. And now there's Mary expecting too. He will have had two new babies in the space of six months. Think of it. Who knows how many more there will be.

MRS GODWIN. Leave us, Fanny. Please.

FANNY *stands*.

JANE. Oh, Fanny, could you find my pink dress for me? And some clean stockings? I can't tell you how I need them.

FANNY. Yes. All right.

FANNY *leaves*.

JANE. I'm sorry you have been unwell, Mama. You really mustn't fret on my account. I'm perfectly happy – as you see.

MRS GODWIN. I will do my very best to express myself in… (*Cannot finish the sentence.*)

JANE. What?

MRS GODWIN.…in a reasonable fashion, as Mr Godwin would say.

JANE. Really, Mama. If you're going to tell me that I should…

MRS GODWIN. When I was not much older than you are, I was seduced. Used. By a man who should have known better.

JANE. Do you mean Charles's father? My father? But he married you. You can hardly say he 'seduced' you when…

MRS GODWIN. No, he did not. And he wasn't your father.
When he discovered that I was expecting your brother, he paid
me to go away from him. He wanted nothing to do with me.

JANE. So... who was my father? You always made me think
that...

MRS GODWIN. Your father was a country squire. Rotten
through and through. He took advantage of my desperate
situation – of my poverty. He treated me like so much dirt
under his shoe. When you were born, he would not even
accept that you were his. When you were three months old,
we were in prison. You were too young to have remembered
it, thank God.

JANE. In prison for what?

MRS GODWIN. Debt, of course. What else? Debt. Debt. Always
debt! I did everything I could to get you out of there. Filthy,
squalid place. You caught a fever and almost died. Then one of
the other women was released and she took you out, and
Charles, and kept you safe until I could come for you.

JANE. I don't believe this. You're making this up.

MRS GODWIN. Do you really think I would make up such a
dreadful, shameful tale? I had hoped to never tell you this. It
has taken me years, years to make some sort of life for
myself and for you. You cannot know what I have endured.
And now you are making exactly the same mistakes I made.

JANE. No, I am not. My situation is completely different.

MRS GODWIN. Another young girl whose life is ruined. Over.

JANE. Oh, don't be so ridiculous...

MRS GODWIN. You are fallen. Tainted. The one fate I prayed
you would never have to suffer.

JANE. You have no idea of the delicacy, the beauty of the
relationship I...

MRS GODWIN. Nobody decent will ever come near you now.
You have lost all chance of a normal, decent match...

JANE. Mr Godwin married you, it seems.

MRS GODWIN. There are not many like Mr Godwin in the world. And Shelley isn't going to marry you, is he? Well, is he?

I want you to come home. Immediately. If you come now, we can say that you went with Mary in order to look after her – to try to bring her home.

JANE. Shelley said that you would do this. He said you would do anything to make me stay here.

MRS GODWIN. Shelley? 'Shelley said…' Why do you listen to him and not to me?

JANE *stands*.

I'm your mother! Why would you doubt that I want what's best for you? When have I done anything which isn't best for you?

JANE. I won't be coming back, Mama.

MRS GODWIN. Oh, you silly, foolish girl!

JANE. I detest this place. I hadn't realised how much I detest it until now. I shall collect my things and then I shall go.

MRS GODWIN. Jane…

JANE. And it's not Jane any more. It's Claire. Jane is such a very dull name. Claire is romantic. Shelley thinks so.

JANE *leaves*.

Scene Six

Night. The living room. The lodgings in Marylebone. JANE *is sobbing.* SHELLEY *is with her.*

SHELLEY. It's all right. It's all right, now.

What did your mother say to you?

JANE *cannot answer.*

You seemed so cheerful when you got back – we thought it
must have gone well.

She shakes her head.

Did Godwin come home? Did he see you?

JANE. No.

SHELLEY. It was brave of you to go. I can't imagine what your
mother thinks to achieve by making you wretched.

JANE. You won't abandon me, will you?

SHELLEY. Abandon you? Is that what she said I would do?

JANE. You won't give me money to make me go away from
you?

SHELLEY. Forgive me, but your mother can be very foolish
sometimes. Jane…

JANE. Claire.

SHELLEY. Claire…

JANE. I don't want to be alone. I don't think I'd be very good
at it.

SHELLEY. You can stay with Mary and I for as long as you
like.

JANE. Can I?

SHELLEY. Oh, I don't even see it like that. We're all together
because we want to be. And while we want to be, we must be
together.

JANE. Yes.

SHELLEY. There are no rules. No demands. No promises. Only
what we want. What we all want.

Pause.

JANE. Do I matter?

SHELLEY. Of course you matter.

JANE. Do I matter to you?

SHELLEY. Yes.

JANE. Can I touch you?

She reaches out and touches him.

I have always longed to touch you. Sometimes, when I've been lying on the end of your bed, my hand has fallen very close to you. Close to your skin. And I've imagined… what it would be like… to touch you. And it's like this. Touch me. Please.

She takes hold of his hand and puts it against her body. They kiss. They stare into each other's eyes – a suspended moment. MARY *enters from the bedroom.*

MARY. What's going on?

SHELLEY. I heard her crying. She's been very upset by her visit this afternoon.

JANE. I'm sorry. I didn't mean to wake you up. I know you need your sleep, Mary.

Pause.

SHELLEY. I think we all need some sleep.

JANE. Can I come in your room?

MARY. No. I think you should stay in here. It's hard enough for me to get comfortable as it is.

SHELLEY. We could probably manage, couldn't we? I could always sleep on the floor…

MARY. No. (*Suddenly gasping with pain.*) Ah!

SHELLEY. Mary?

MARY. Ah! Oh! That's… Ah!

SHELLEY. Mary, what it is it?

MARY. Something's… Oh!

JANE. Is it the baby?

SHELLEY. Do you need to sit…?

MARY. No. No. No. Oh, my Lord…

JANE. Is it the baby? It can't be the baby, can it? It's too soon.

MARY *takes deep breaths*.

SHELLEY. Is it easing? Mary?

JANE. Perhaps you should go for the doctor?

MARY. I've never felt anything quite so... Do you think it's the
    baby? Could it be?

SHELLEY. I don't know. Do you think it is?

MARY. I think it might be.

JANE. Shall I do something?

MARY. Go away.

JANE. My goodness. You're very stern this evening...

MARY. Just go away! Ah! It's coming again. Shelley!

SHELLEY. That's it. I'll hold you, shall I?

JANE. Shall I go for the landlady? She might know a midwife.

MARY. It's too soon. I'm frightened.

SHELLEY. Try to keep calm. It might not come.

MARY. Shelley...

SHELLEY. Oh, my poor darling...

MARY. If I die...

SHELLEY. You won't. You won't die.

MARY. But I might. I might.

Scene Seven

*Day. The lodgings. MARY is lying on the daybed, sleeping.
FANNY is sitting close to her, with a baby in her arms. MARY
opens her eyes.*

FANNY. Hello, clever little sister.

MARY. How long have you been here?

FANNY. Not long.

MARY. I wanted you to come. I kept asking for you.

FANNY. I know. I came as soon as we got the news.

MARY. Is Father going to come?

FANNY. No. No. But he allowed me to, and that's something, isn't it?

She's beautiful.

MARY. She's very small.

FANNY. But she's perfect.

MARY. Shelley says she's alert. It's so hard – I don't have anything to compare her with.

FANNY. She's certainly looking about. (*To baby.*) Aren't you, little one?

(*To* MARY.) How are you feeling?

MARY. I'm fine. Truly. I'm certainly not going to spend another day lying down. Tomorrow we shall both be up and dressed and taking our first walk.

FANNY. Are you sure you ought to?

MARY. I don't hold with all this lying-in. Neither does Shelley. Mother didn't.

FANNY. No.

MARY. And we need some fresh air. It's damp in this place.

FANNY *passes* MARY *a small bundle of baby clothes.*

FANNY. Here. They're from Mama – Mrs Godwin. I think they must have been Jane's.

MARY *looks at the clothes.*

It's kind of her, isn't it? She cares more than you think she does.

MARY. More than he does, apparently.

FANNY. Mary…

MARY. What did he say – when he heard she'd been born? He didn't say anything, did he?

FANNY. He said you'd had a girl. And then he said that I could come and see you if I wished.

That was his present, in a way.

Things are very hard for him at the moment…

MARY. You know, I really think he doesn't care. Not in a real way. All those times when he was cold and distant from us, and I used to think it didn't matter, because deep down, there was this… bedrock of love. But now I don't think there is. If I can do one thing, one thing he doesn't approve of and yet he can't forgive me.

FANNY. Perhaps we shouldn't talk about this now.

MARY. I know what he thinks: that I've betrayed my gifts – my promise – but he's so wrong. Because this is it – I'm living out my promise. I'm living the life with Shelley that he and my mother dreamt of living. Does he think I've just thrown everything up to swoon about like some lovesick girl? I'm reading and learning and thinking and writing more than I've ever done. (*Pointing to the books beside her.*) Look. Look at all these. I've read them all. And Shelley and I talk about them. Talk and talk like I used to do with him. I want you to tell him that. Make him see that.

FANNY. I'll try. He's… He has a lot of worries at the moment.

MARY. I don't care. She's his first grandchild.

FANNY. We have to sell the business. He's desperately trying to find a buyer. One of his creditors has taken him to court. If we can't find the money, we'll be made bankrupt. I'm sorry. I wasn't going to tell you today.

JANE *and* SHELLEY *enter.* JANE *is carrying a cake.* SHELLEY *imitates a trumpet fanfare.*

JANE. We present… the cake!

MARY *and* FANNY *laugh.*

MARY. How did you manage that?

SHELLEY. The mother of a friend. She never could resist me.

JANE. We're going to go down and make some tea, and find some plates, and…

SHELLEY. And have a party.

JANE. Shelley has written a song for Clara. It's so funny. I'm going to sing it.

SHELLEY. We won't be long. Don't even think about leaving, Fanny.

JANE *and* SHELLEY *leave.* MARY *and* FANNY *smile at each other.*

MARY (*of the baby*). She's called Clara.

FANNY. Shelley told me.

MARY. Jane has started saying that she wants to be called Claire.

FANNY. Yes.

MARY. I didn't let that put me off. She knows it's always been my favourite name. She copies everything I do. It's insufferable.

FANNY. I remember when we used to sit in the graveyard and talk about what our daughters would be called. Yours was always Clara.

MARY. And yours was Mary.

FANNY. And now look…

She smiles down at the baby.

MARY. I'll try to do something to help Papa.

FANNY. Don't think about that now.

MARY. I'll talk to Shelley. I'll try.

Scene Eight

The parlour. Skinner Street. GODWIN *and* MRS GODWIN *are with* FANNY.

MRS GODWIN. But I don't understand. How can Shelley pay our debts when he hasn't got any money himself?

FANNY. He has looked into the possibility of selling another bond – a post-obit bond. But the sums he was offered were derisory.

GODWIN. I told him we were fortunate the first time.

FANNY. So, what he is proposing is that he goes to our more serious creditors and offers to… to take on our debts. He will promise to pay them what we owe, as soon as he inherits some money. And he'll offer them a considerable sum of interest besides.

MRS GODWIN. Well… will they accept that?

GODWIN. Yes. Most likely. It would be a far better bet than a claim against a failing business.

MRS GODWIN. Then we must accept his offer.

FANNY. You would not have to do anything, Papa. You would not have to be present at any of the meetings. I can liaise with Shelley.

MRS GODWIN. Well, I think it is a very fair offer. And certainly no more than he owes us.

GODWIN. If I accept this offer, Mrs Godwin, it will not be because of anything we are 'owed'. It will be on exactly the same basis as our last arrangement. A philosophical basis. *Political Justice*.

MRS GODWIN. Oh, no one really believed that in the first place. It's all over the city that you sold your daughters – one for eight hundred and the other for seven.

GODWIN. How dare you repeat that in this house?

MRS GODWIN. You must face facts, Mr Godwin. And the fact is that we have no earthly option but to accept.

Pause.

FANNY. I'll leave you to think about it.

MRS GODWIN. There's nothing to think about. If you don't accept this offer, Mr Godwin, I shall...

GODWIN. You shall die. Yes, yes, Mrs Godwin. You have been tantalising us with the promise of your demise for several months now and yet here you are, as large as life.

MRS GODWIN. How cruel. You are a very cruel man.

She begins to cry, and leaves. FANNY *and* GODWIN *are silent for a few moments.*

FANNY. They really want to help.

GODWIN. You may tell Mr Shelley that I accept his offer.

FANNY. Right. Good.

GODWIN. You may also tell him that there will be no word of thanks from me. Nor will this form the basis of a reconciliation.

FANNY. As you wish.

The baby is adorable. And Mary's writing and reading a great deal. She wanted you to know...

GODWIN *walks out.*

Scene Nine

Night. The lodgings. SHELLEY *and* JANE *enter.* SHELLEY *is holding a candlestick. They do not notice, at first, that* MARY *is kneeling in the middle of the floor.*

SHELLEY. But an audience doesn't want an actor to bludgeon them about the the head like that.

JANE. He was loud, I agree, but he was very imposing. Isn't that what the character required?

SHELLEY. He certainly imposed upon me – for two and a half hours.

JANE (*laughing*). You're terrible.

SHELLEY. We'd better be quiet.

JANE. Yes.

> JANE *suddenly catches sight of* MARY *and lets out a little shriek.*

Oh, Mary. You gave me such a fright!

SHELLEY. What's wrong?

MARY. She's dead.

> MARY's *gaze moves to a chair, where she has left the swaddled baby.* SHELLEY *walks over to the chair, and kneeling down, touches the baby's face.*

I went to wake her for her last feed, and she was like that.

SHELLEY. Oh, no.

MARY. I don't know why. She had been so happy today.

JANE (*approaching* SHELLEY). Are you sure she's…? I mean…?

SHELLEY. Jane, no. No. She's gone.

> SHELLEY *goes to* MARY *and puts his arms around her.*

MARY. I'm sorry.

> SHELLEY *sobs.*

Scene Ten

Late evening. The parlour. Skinner Street. Outside, a thunder storm is raging. FANNY *arrives home. She is soaked to the skin, and exhausted.* GODWIN *enters from his study.*

GODWIN. Could they not have put you in a carriage?

FANNY. I was wet when I arrived there. It made no difference. Besides, they have just as little money as we do.

GODWIN. I'm sure Shelley could run to the cost of a carriage.

FANNY. Shelley wasn't there.

GODWIN. Oh?

FANNY. He's had to stay away from the house for a few days. One of his creditors isn't prepared to wait. There's a warrant out for his arrest.

GODWIN. I see.

FANNY. He and Mary have been meeting in the cathedral.

GODWIN. Sanctuary.

FANNY. Yes. It's a terrible shame. Just when she has such need of him. I told her she should speak to the creditor and explain what's happened. Surely he would show a little compassion?

GODWIN. The world does not stop turning because of the death of one child. Nor should it.

FANNY *looks at him in dismay.* MRS GODWIN *enters.*

MRS GODWIN. So, you're back then.

FANNY. Yes.

MRS GODWIN. Couldn't they have put you in a carriage?

FANNY. I didn't mind.

MRS GODWIN. I don't know why you had to go in the first place. She's got Jane to comfort her.

FANNY. She asked for me. She wanted me. I should have gone days ago.

MRS GODWIN. And how is madam?

FANNY. Oh, please don't do that!

MRS GODWIN. I beg your pardon?

FANNY. Mary is… coping. She's sad. Bereft. But she's trying very hard. She's reading Shakespeare, Papa. Just like you always do when things are… dreadful. Papa, please, please go and see her.

MRS GODWIN. Oh, you silly girl.

FANNY. It would mean so much to her. Or write to her at least. If you could only see how bewildered she is… how shocked…

MRS GODWIN. And that's supposed to be our fault, is it?

FANNY. They have done so much to make amends. Taken on our debts…

GODWIN. Please be quiet.

FANNY. I'm sorry. It's just…

FANNY *does not dare to go on.*

MRS GODWIN. Of course, there are some would say that they brought this on themselves. With their sinfulness.

FANNY. Who would say that?

MRS GODWIN. Some would say it is God's punishment.

GODWIN. Please do not introduce hocus-pocus into the equation.

MRS GODWIN. I'm only saying what others will say.

GODWIN. Go and change out of those wet things, Fanny. The last thing we need is for you to catch a cold.

FANNY *leaves.*

Scene Eleven

Night. The lodgings. The storm is still overhead. MARY, *alone on the daybed, is dreaming. The book she was reading has fallen from her hands.*

She dreams that SHELLEY *is there, with the baby's body in his arms.*

SHELLEY. Quickly, Mary. Come closer to the fire. We must make her warm.

MARY *goes to him. They crouch by the fire.*

We can bring her back to life.

MARY. Can we?

SHELLEY. We can breathe the life back into her. Breathe on her, like this.

They begin to breathe over the baby's body.

Look – she's stirring. Life and death are nothing, Mary. They are the same.

MARY. She's breathing. Clara? Clara? Clara?

MARY *wakes up suddenly.*

Clara?

She realises that she has been dreaming. She begins to cry. JANE *comes out of the bedroom and sees her.*

She goes to her and puts her arms around her.

JANE. Oh, don't, Mary. Don't cry.

Scene Twelve

A graveyard. It's snowing. MARY *and* SHELLEY *are muffled up against the cold. They stand, hand in hand, looking down at the baby's grave. It is marked by a small, simple headstone.*

MARY (*reading*). 'Clara Shelley.'

SHELLEY. It's all I could afford. Is it all right?

MARY. Yes. Yes. Of course it is. What else is there to say?

Pause.

SHELLEY. Mary, I got a letter from my father's lawyer today. It seems my grandfather has died.

MARY. Your grandfather? I'm so sorry.

SHELLEY. My father inherits the estate, of course. But he wants to come to an arrangement with me – a financial arrangement. Mary, it means we will soon have money. As much money as we need.

MARY. I see.

SHELLEY. And I can help so many people. Do so much good.

MARY. Yes.

SHELLEY. I can help your father. And Harriet – she needs more money for the children.

MARY. Yes.

SHELLEY. I've been thinking: we should go abroad. Leave England. Or at least make plans to. It will be some time before the money is mine.

MARY. How long?

SHELLEY. Two months? Three? But as soon as we have it, we should go and live somewhere beautiful. Somewhere inspiring. Away from all the distractions and the disapproval.

MARY. Somewhere we can write.

SHELLEY. Yes. Yes.

MARY. What about Jane?

SHELLEY. I thought Jane could come with us. Mary darling, it isn't good for two people to be always together. Forced in upon each other...

MARY. You make it sound like a form of torture.

SHELLEY. We should take whoever wants to come. And we will meet people there, I'm sure. We will form a community of like-minded people.

MARY. Then tell Jane your heart is mine. Your heart is mine alone. Make her understand that.

SHELLEY. I will then. Because it's true.

Let's walk home through the snow.

MARY. Yes.

They leave the graveyard. GODWIN *suddenly walks into view.* MARY *sees him and turns pale.*

(*Quietly.*) My father.

GODWIN, *closer now, sees them and stops.*

SHELLEY. Godwin. This is a fortuitous...

GODWIN *walks past them, without looking at them. He is gone.*

MARY. My father...

End of Act Three.

ACT FOUR

Scene One

A hot, late-summer's day. GODWIN's study. Skinner Street. Sun is pouring through the windows. GODWIN enters. He has been out, and is very hot and exhausted. He sits down and puts down the newspaper he is carrying. He loosens his collar, wipes the sweat from his brow. FANNY hurries in.

FANNY. Papa?

GODWIN. This summer seems to be going on forever.

FANNY. Are you unwell?

GODWIN. A little, perhaps.

FANNY pours him a glass of water from a carafe.

Thank you.

It seems I am a radical designed for moderate climates.

FANNY waits until he has recovered a little.

FANNY. Did you see my aunts?

GODWIN. Yes. We had an hour together.

FANNY. Are they going to come here?

GODWIN. Sit down, Fanny.

She does so. She stares at him, expectantly.

Fanny... your aunts are no longer prepared to have you at the school in Dublin.

FANNY. Why?

GODWIN. I'm sure you can imagine why. They read the newspapers like everybody else. They have read about your sisters' latest exploits with Lord Byron in Switzerland. They are very angry. They believe, with some justification, that the family connection is damaging their school's reputation.

FANNY. But surely they don't believe those reports? You don't believe them?

GODWIN. I don't know what to believe.

FANNY. I have had several letters from Mary. They have made Lord Byron's acquaintance – that much is true. They happen to have taken villas close to each other. It would be strange if they had not become friends. But anything else is simply scurrilous gossip. The newspapers will say anything about Lord Byron…

GODWIN. And about Shelley. And about your sisters, it appears. (*Taking up the newspaper.*) There is another tale in here today. A gentleman has returned from travelling in the Alps, to say that 'he saw Lord Byron being rowed across a lake in Geneva, dressed in flowing robes, like a latter-day Caesar, and with those two wicked women dancing attendance upon him.' They do not give your sisters' names. They content themselves with saying that they are my daughters – 'daughters of the infamous radical, William Godwin.'

FANNY. But it's nonsense. It must be. They probably simply went for a row on the lake. People see what they want to see.

GODWIN. Your aunts have accepted that Mary has entered into a liaison, albeit unconventional, with Shelley. They seem more concerned about Jane. Her position is certainly more spurious. They wanted an assurance that I would never allow Jane to return to this house.

FANNY. But why would Jane return here? Even if she does, it won't be for months – years perhaps.

GODWIN. On the contrary, I think they will return to England in the very near future. According to my lawyer, Shelley is being urgently petitioned to return. He needs to be here to conclude the dealings with his father. It was madness for them to leave when they did. If Jane were to ask to return here, I would not be able to refuse her. For Mrs Godwin's sake.

Pause.

Your aunts' is not the only school. We could consider placing you elsewhere.

FANNY. Where? Who would have me?

GODWIN. I will make enquiries. Please give it some consideration.

FANNY. I know I must find the means to pay my way. As Mama says, you cannot support me forever.

GODWIN. I will support you for as long as it takes.

Now. Shall we have some tea?

FANNY *stands*.

New dress, is it?

FANNY. It's one of Mary's old ones. I wanted to look tidy – for my aunts.

GODWIN. It looks very well on you.

FANNY. It suited Mary better.

Scene Two

Two months later. The drawing room of SHELLEY*'s house in Bath. It is a bright, airy room, filled with fine furniture.* MARY *is sitting at a desk, writing.*

SHELLEY (*off*). Mary!

MARY. Here!

SHELLEY *rushes in*.

SHELLEY. Mary…

MARY. You're back. And sooner than I'd hoped.

SHELLEY (*kissing her*). Hello, my darling.

MARY. How did you fare? What did the lawyer say?

SHELLEY. I'll tell you all about it soon. But first I have a surprise for you. Close your eyes.

MARY. What sort of a surprise?

SHELLEY. Close your eyes. Something I found on the street.

MARY closes her eyes. SHELLEY beckons to FANNY to enter. She does so. She is dressed for travelling and carries a small bag.

MARY. Oh, no. It's not a dog, or a cat, is it? We can't…

SHELLEY. Open them.

MARY opens her eyes and sees FANNY.

MARY. Fanny! Fanny…

FANNY. Hello, Mary dear.

MARY rushes to her and they embrace.

MARY. My darling, darling girl. But what are you doing in Bath?

FANNY. I hope you don't mind. You said I should come and visit.

MARY. How did you get here?

FANNY. The stagecoach. I travelled overnight. It's not so very far from London.

SHELLEY. I was on my way home in the carriage, and I saw this figure standing in the square by the Pump House, looking about as though she had landed on a distant planet. And then I thought – that's a very familiar figure.

FANNY. I would have found the right street eventually.

MARY. My dear girl. Sit down, you must be exhausted.

SHELLEY. If only I'd known – you could have travelled with me.

FANNY. I didn't know you were in London.

MARY. He's there far too often at the moment.

FANNY. Where's the new baby? I'm longing to see him.

MARY. He's asleep. We can't wake him. Nurse would be livid. It took her an age to get him down. He hates to sleep.

SHELLEY. You shall see him as soon as he's awake. He's beautiful.

MARY. He looks like his father.

SHELLEY. Like his mother.

MARY. We call him Wilmouse. Did I tell you that in my letter?

FANNY. No.

SHELLEY. He's a soft, downy, curious creature.

MARY. You'll adore him. And he'll adore you.

FANNY. And he's well? Quite well?

MARY. Yes. He is.

FANNY. I'm so glad for you.

MARY *takes her hand.*

MARY. I can't believe you're real.

FANNY. What a lovely house this is.

SHELLEY. We were lucky to find it at short notice. We've taken it for three months.

MARY. We have servants, can you believe it?

SHELLEY. Well-paid servants, I should add, who have two days off a week.

FANNY. Of course.

MARY. And we brought William's nurse with us from Switzerland. And I'm managing to get lots of work done.

SHELLEY. Mary's writing a novel.

FANNY. Good.

SHELLEY. It's exceptional. It's going to astonish the world.

MARY. There's still a lot of work to do.

SHELLEY. And I'm writing another poem. It's almost finished.

FANNY. I'm glad you're both writing. It's what you ought to do.

So you don't mean to stay in Bath for long?

MARY. No. We shall go back to Geneva as soon as we can. We love it there.

FANNY. Yes. Your letters have been making me quite jealous.

SHELLEY. A few more meetings with the lawyers and we shall be gone. I hope your father got the cheque I sent to him last week?

FANNY. Yes. He did. Thank you.

SHELLEY. Once things have been properly settled, I will be able to give him a more substantial sum.

FANNY. I'm afraid he couldn't cash the cheque.

SHELLEY. Oh?

FANNY. You… made it out to him. His name. Perhaps you've forgotten – he can't be seen to be accepting money from you. Not with…

SHELLEY. Ah.

FANNY. If you could make a cheque out to his lawyer, then he…

SHELLEY. Yes. Of course.

MARY. So much for honest transactions.

FANNY. I'm sorry. We do really need the money…

SHELLEY. I shall send a cheque to his lawyer.

FANNY. Thank you.

MARY. So how are things at Skinner Street?

FANNY. I don't want to talk about Skinner Street. Not now. If you don't mind?

How's Jane? Where is she?

MARY *and* SHELLEY *glance at each other.*

SHELLEY. I… think…

MARY. She's lying down.

SHELLEY. I'll go and fetch her, shall I, Mary?

MARY. Yes. She'll want to know that Fanny's here.

SHELLEY. And I'll look in on William. I'll make as much
noise as I can.

He leaves.

FANNY. It's wonderful to see you so happy.

MARY. There's something I should tell you about Claire – Jane.
She's having a baby. That's partly why we came to Bath and
not to London. No one must know. Not yet, at least.

FANNY. You aren't serious?

MARY. There's no need for anyone to make a fuss about it. It's
perfectly natural.

FANNY. Whose is it? Is it his? Is it Shelley's?

MARY. Shelley's? No. Why on earth would you say that? The
father is…

FANNY. Is it Lord Byron?

MARY. Yes.

FANNY. Oh, my God…

MARY. It was… unexpected. But it has happened. It's
happening. We're glad. Another addition to our family.

FANNY. When… will it be born?

MARY. Around Christmas time, we think.

She met Lord Byron in London. Before we even went to
Geneva. I don't know what possessed her – well, I do. She
wrote to him at Drury Lane. His play was being performed
there. She said she wanted to become an actress – as though
she isn't an actress already. She begged him to help her. She
went to see him. Met him in one of the dressing rooms.
Anyway… she introduced us to him. He adores Shelley, as
you can imagine. They argue – but they love to argue. When
Byron said he was going to Geneva, we decided to go too.
We had been planning to go abroad.

It's sad, in a way. When he found out about the baby, he was
horrified. He doesn't care for Claire. He doesn't even like
her. He treats her with contempt. Plays tricks on her. Makes
her a fool.

JANE *enters*.

JANE. Fanny! Dearest sister! What a wonderful surprise.

FANNY. Hello…

JANE. And now you know my surprise. Isn't it thrilling? Has Mary told you who the father is?

FANNY. Yes.

JANE. You see – she has her poet and now I have mine. Isn't it funny? And mine is the most notorious poet in the whole world! But you mustn't tell Mama. Or Papa. We shall tell them when the time is right. Shan't we, Mary? How is Mama? As dreadful as ever, I suppose?

FANNY. I… I don't know.

JANE. You don't know? Haven't you come from Skinner Street?

FANNY (*standing*). I think I should go.

JANE. Go? But…

MARY. Don't be silly, Fanny. Sit down.

FANNY. I… There's a coach on the hour. I should be able to catch it if I leave now.

JANE. But you've only just arrived.

FANNY. Yes. But… it was a mistake… for me to come.

JANE. Why? Fanny…?

MARY. Let her go. She clearly can't bear to spend another moment in this house of iniquity.

FANNY. That isn't what…

MARY. Yes, it is. She has spent too long with Mrs Godwin.

FANNY. I'm not judging you.

MARY. Yes you are. You're judging Jane and you're judging me. You always have done.

JANE. Really, Fanny. Surely you're not so 'worldly' that you object to having babies out of wedlock? You were born out of wedlock. Or have you forgotten that?

FANNY. That's not what…

MARY. What then? Just say it. Say what it is you wish to say.

FANNY. I just wish you would… think about others a little before you act. Think about the effect on others.

FANNY has tears in her eyes. MARY can see her distress.

JANE. We can't spend all our lives thinking about everybody else! In my opinion, the greatest sin in this world is sitting around your whole life and waiting for things to happen. Far too many women do that. Waiting, waiting, hour after hour and day after day.

FANNY. And that's what you think I do, I suppose?

JANE. Yes. Yes, I do.

FANNY. You don't think I have dreams and ambitions like you do? You don't think I want to walk in the sunlight, and write or… paint, or…

JANE. Well, it doesn't seem so. Because you don't do anything.

MARY. Don't, Jane. That's enough.

JANE. You're too busy running about, doing as you're told, trying to keep everyone happy, happy, happy. Well, life isn't like that.

FANNY stares down at the floor.

MARY. Please sit down, Fanny. At least stay tonight. Stay and meet William.

JANE. You're Mary Wollstonecraft's daughter. Doesn't that mean anything to you?

FANNY. It means a great deal.

MARY. Fanny…

JANE. Well, she wouldn't look down her nose at us. She wouldn't judge us. She'd be proud of the way we're living. Wouldn't she, Mary?

SHELLEY enters. He looks at them all with bewildered concern.

FANNY. I think I should go.

She takes up her bag and leaves the room.

Scene Three

A street, Bath. FANNY *and* SHELLEY *arrive at the place where the coach stops.*

SHELLEY. Ten minutes to spare.

FANNY. Thank you for walking with me. You should go back now.

SHELLEY. No. I'll wait for the coach.

FANNY. I'd rather be alone. Please.

SHELLEY. I'm not going to leave you like this.

FANNY. I'm not fit company. For anyone.

SHELLEY. Fanny. Fanny, this is madness. Why don't you come and live with us? Come back to Geneva with us. Whole new worlds, new vistas would open up to you. You don't realise… I don't think you realise how trapped you are.

FANNY. Oh, I do.

SHELLEY. Then come to us. Leave Godwin and come to us.

Pause.

FANNY. In here – (*Shows him her bag.*) I have a nightdress, and a hairbrush and a change of clothes. I wanted to stay.

SHELLEY. Then stay.

FANNY. In all my letters to Geneva, I tried to make it clear… how much I wanted to come to you, to be with you all. It frightened me a little, the thought of it, but I decided to put my fears aside. And every time Mary wrote to me I would hope, hope to see those words – 'come to us'.

SHELLEY. And I'm saying them now. Dear Fanny, come to us.

FANNY. I can't. Even if I thought that Mary wanted it, I can't come to you. I can't live the way you live. I realise that now. Because I don't think it's right. There. I've said it. You can put me in a box with the reactionaries and the cowards and push us out to sea. People get hurt. Children get hurt. Children grow up feeling unloved, unvalued. Out of place.

SHELLEY. William won't feel unloved.

FANNY. I know that...

SHELLEY. I will love and care for all my children. I've asked Harriet for custody of our son.

FANNY. And what of Ianthe? Have you asked for her?

SHELLEY. I...

FANNY. And why should Harriet have to give up her child?

SHELLEY. I ask her, repeatedly, to come and join us...

FANNY. This isn't... I'm not judging you. I just know that I cannot live as you live. I want you all to be happy.

SHELLEY. We only have one life, Fanny. We must make use of every second. The powers that be – the rich, the government, society – they do everything they can to close us down, to shackle us... We have to live bravely. We have to strive towards enlightenment. You have so much to offer to the world...

FANNY. Don't. Please. I can't bear any more.

SHELLEY. Fanny...

FANNY. I'm tired. Will you go now? Please?

SHELLEY. What if I went to sit on those steps over there...?

FANNY. No.

SHELLEY *resigns himself to leaving.*

SHELLEY. I'll write to you.

FANNY *nods.*

He kisses her hand. He leaves. FANNY *remains, staring at the ground, for some time. Then she suddenly picks up her bag, and walks away into the streets.*

Scene Four

Bath. MARY *dreams of* FANNY. FANNY *is climbing onto the edge of a bridge over a river – just as her mother did. She jumps. She is overwhelmed by the water.*

MARY (*calling out*). Give me your hand! I'm here! Reach out to me! Reach out to me!

Scene Five

A room at an inn in Swansea. Night. A MAID, *carrying a candle, shows* FANNY *into the room.* FANNY *takes in the simple bed, the small table beside it. She puts her bag down.*

MAID. Will there be anything else, miss?

FANNY. No, thank you. I shall see to the candle myself.

MAID (*handing her the candle*). I'll bid you goodnight then, miss.

FANNY *hands the* MAID *a coin.*

Oh. Thank you, miss.

FANNY. Goodnight.

The MAID *leaves.* FANNY *stands still.*

In GODWIN's *study at Skinner Street,* GODWIN *is trying to immerse himself in Shakespeare.* MRS GODWIN *rushes in. She is holding a letter in her hand.*

MRS GODWIN. A letter from Fanny.

GODWIN. Are you sure?

He jumps up and takes the letter.

Thank heavens.

He opens it.

MRS GODWIN. Posted in Bristol.

GODWIN. Then she isn't with them.

MRS GODWIN. What is she doing in Bristol? Do we know anyone in Bristol?

GODWIN is reading the letter. His legs almost give way beneath him.

What is it? What does it say?

GODWIN. No. No.

In the room at the inn, FANNY places the candle on the small table. She sits down on the bed. She takes off her hat and her jacket, and places them neatly on the end of the bed. She unpins her hair and lets it down.

In the drawing room in Bath, MARY opens a letter from FANNY. She gasps. SHELLEY enters and goes to her.

SHELLEY. Mary?

MARY. Oh, my God. Oh, my God...

He takes the letter from her and reads.

SHELLEY. I'll leave at once.

MARY. I'm coming with you.

SHELLEY. No. It will take too long in the carriage. I'll ride. Help me get my things together.

He rushes to the door. MARY is rooted to the spot.

Mary!

She goes after him.

In the room at the inn, FANNY opens her bag and takes out a bottle of laudanum. She puts it in her lap. Then she takes out a folded note, and opening it out, reads it quietly.

FANNY. 'I have long determined that the best thing I could do was to put an end to the existence of a being whose birth was unfortunate, and whose life has only been a series of pain to those persons who have hurt their health in endeavouring to promote her welfare. Perhaps to hear of my death will give you pain, but you will soon have the blessing of forgetting that such a creature ever existed as Fanny.'

She stares at the note for a moment, then folds it again, and places it on the table. Then she takes up the bottle of laudanum, opens it, and drinks from it, in longer and longer draughts.

She puts it on the table. She blows out the candle. She lies down on the bed, and closes her eyes.

Scene Six

Day. The inn at Swansea. The MAID leads SHELLEY to the bedroom.

MAID. This is the room, sir. The coroner said he would take the body to the poor house if we needed it, but we didn't like to send her there. She seemed a very sweet lady.

SHELLEY. Can we go in?

The MAID leads him into the room. FANNY's body is on the bed. SHELLEY stares at her.

MAID. Do you know her, sir? Is she the one you're looking for?

SHELLEY picks up the note from the table, and reads it.

SHELLEY. Who else has seen this note?

MAID. The coroner. The man from the newspaper.

SHELLEY tears off the name from it.

Sir – the coroner said we should leave things just as they are until he comes back…

SHELLEY *gives her a sovereign.*

SHELLEY. I don't want anyone else to know this name.

MAID. But it'll be in the paper tomorrow most likely.

SHELLEY. I'll speak to the paper. And to the coroner.

MAID. Yes, sir. No use in adding to her shame. You know her then? I don't mean to speak out of turn, sir, but if you do, you should claim her body. Else it'll be a pauper's grave. And she'll not be long in the ground before the robbers come. They always take the ones who no one misses.

SHELLEY *touches* FANNY*'s face. Then he hurries from the room.*

Scene Seven

The parlour. Skinner Street. MRS GODWIN *accompanies* GODWIN *into the room.* GODWIN *has just arrived home. He is ashen-faced and exhausted. He slumps into a chair. He looks up at* MRS GODWIN, *and shakes his head.*

GODWIN. Too late.

I got to Bristol and made enquiries. But she'd already left. She'd gone on to Swansea. She went there with her aunts once, do you remember?

MRS GODWIN. Yes.

GODWIN. I was going to follow her, but then someone came in on the coach from Swansea with a newspaper. It said the body of a fair-haired young woman had been found.

She'd left a note. There was no name.

MRS GODWIN (*upset*). The stupid girl. Why would she do such a thing?

GODWIN. I must write to Mary and Shelley.

MRS GODWIN (*surprised*). Write to them?

GODWIN. Yes. I must tell them not to go to Swansea. If this gets out… the scandal would be catastrophic. We must all stay away from Swansea.

How I wish… she had told me… how she was feeling.

MRS GODWIN. She was her mother's daughter. It was in the blood.

GODWIN. She was a dear… dear girl. Fanny.

He breaks down in tears. MRS GODWIN *kneels beside him and holds him.*

MRS GODWIN. Oh, Mr Godwin. Don't. Oh, my poor, poor love. My poor love.

In Bath, MARY *is waiting, with the baby in her arms.* JANE *is standing close by.* SHELLEY *enters and walks towards* MARY. *He puts his arms around her.* JANE *begins to cry.*

SHELLEY. She was buried in a churchyard. It's a peaceful spot. It was the least that I could do for her.

JANE comes to them and puts her arms around them as best she can. They are locked in grief.

End of Act Four.

ACT FIVE

Scene One

The parlour. Skinner Street. MRS GODWIN *leads* SHELLEY *into the room.* SHELLEY *looks pale and serious.*

MRS GODWIN. Please come in.

Please sit down. Would you care for some tea?

SHELLEY. No, thank you.

SHELLEY *looks about the room. It is over two years since he has been here.* FANNY*'s shawl is lying on the back of a chair.*

MRS GODWIN. I was very sorry to hear about your wife, Mr Shelley. A terrible affair. And coming so soon after Fanny.

SHELLEY. Yes.

MRS GODWIN. The Serpentine. A public park. Such a strange place to drown oneself. I said to Mr Godwin, I wouldn't have thought there would be sufficient water.

And she was pregnant, they say.

SHELLEY. Yes. I believe so.

MRS GODWIN. Do you know who the father was?

SHELLEY. No. She was living with an army officer, I believe. Or had been.

MRS GODWIN. Well. It doesn't matter now, does it? Another feckless young man, I dare say, who thought nothing of... She must have been quite desperate. Very sad.

SHELLEY. Is Mr Godwin going to see me?

MRS GODWIN. Yes. Yes, I believe he is. I'll ask him to come through. (*Going towards the study.*) He's writing another novel, you know? We have high hopes of it.

(*Pausing.*) How's my Jane?

SHELLEY. She's… she's well. She's quite well.

> MRS GODWIN *goes into the study.* SHELLEY *takes a deep breath to steady himself. He stands and moves about the room. He goes to the chair, and runs his hand over* FANNY's *shawl.*

> GODWIN *enters with* MRS GODWIN. *The two men look at each other for some time.*

Godwin.

GODWIN. Shelley.

Pause.

SHELLEY. I hardly know what to say. It's been a long time.

GODWIN. Yes.

I was sorry to hear about your wife. About Harriet.

SHELLEY. Thank you.

MRS GODWIN. We have just been discussing that. He doesn't know who the father was.

GODWIN. Shelley, I want to thank you, for the letter you wrote to me after Fanny's death. I know I replied rather harshly at the time. I know I said that I could not use your sympathy, but… on reflection… your words meant a great deal to me.

And I want to thank you for your discretion. And for seeing her buried.

SHELLEY. She asked me to bury her. In the letter she sent before she died.

GODWIN. Did she?

SHELLEY. It was all done anonymously.

GODWIN. Yes. No one else knows what happened. If people ask after her, I say that she died of a fever, on her way to see her aunts in Ireland. I think that is best.

SHELLEY. I understand.

Godwin, I've come to tell you that I have asked Mary… to marry me.

MRS GODWIN. Oh! Oh, that is good news. Isn't it, Mr Godwin? And after everything that's happened.

SHELLEY. My views on marriage have not altered. But I am fighting for custody of my two children by Harriet. Her family wish to keep them. I stand little chance of prevailing, if my situation with Mary remains unchanged. And financially, our marriage offers her greater assurance. It is what the law demands, it seems, and so I have decided that I must…

GODWIN. Compromise.

SHELLEY. Yes. On this occasion. Until the law catches up with mankind.

Pause.

MRS GODWIN. Well, that's very good news. Not quite romantic, perhaps, but we are all realists here, I think. Isn't it good news, Mr Godwin?

GODWIN. When shall you be married?

SHELLEY. Soon. At Christmas. We can see no advantage in delay.

Godwin, will you consider attending our wedding?

GODWIN. Yes. I should be delighted.

Scene Two

Day. The vestry of a church. MARY is waiting. SHELLEY enters.

SHELLEY. He's here.

She nods.

Shall we go through?

MARY. No. I have to talk to him. I can't just go in there and take his hand and speak my vows in front of him. Will you ask him to come to me?

SHELLEY. Yes.

MARY. I'm sorry. If you could wait…?

SHELLEY. Of course. I will always be waiting for you, Mary.

He kisses her and leaves. MARY *waits anxiously. After a moment,* GODWIN *enters. Their eyes meet.*

GODWIN. New dress?

MARY. Yes.

GODWIN. Very pretty.

He approaches her. When he reaches her, he isn't sure what to do. He taps her arm, awkwardly, and then moves some distance away from her.

Quite a day, then.

MARY. Yes.

GODWIN. I've just been introduced to my grandson. William. Named for me, I assume?

MARY. Yes. Who else?

GODWIN. He's a fine little chap. Looks like an angel, truth be told.

MARY. He's not an angel. He can be diabolical at times. But we forgive him. We always forgive him.

GODWIN. Yes. I hope you will allow me to become acquainted with him.

MARY. I hope you will.

Pause.

GODWIN. How is your work coming along?

MARY. Very well. I've written a novel. It's almost finished.

GODWIN. A novel, eh?

MARY. I'm going to start looking for a publisher.

GODWIN. And what is your novel about?

MARY. It's about... about a man who is... driven, consumed by the desire to explore the very limits of his powers... of science, of knowledge. He creates a creature... from the parts of other humans. A living being. But when he has created it, he finds he cannot countenance its needs – its need for love, companionship, respect, its whole monstrous reality. It pursues him, across mountains and seas. Across the wide world. They come to hate each other.

I thought of you a lot, while I was writing. All your ideas about... humanity, they have all been there to draw upon. If I ever doubted how much I've learned from you, I do not doubt it now.

GODWIN. And I am the monstrous creator, I suppose?

MARY. I don't know. Perhaps. And which am I?

GODWIN. I should like to read it.

MARY. I'd like that.

GODWIN. I cannot promise to be kind, of course.

MARY. Of course.

Pause.

GODWIN. I've missed you, Mary.

Pause.

MARY. Do you ever think it is a curse – this passion of the mind? This inability to leave the world unfathomed? Because I fear it might be. When I think of Fanny... of how little time I gave to her... how little account I took of her...

GODWIN. Fanny was not strong. She was exceptionally sensitive. I doubt she...

MARY. Then we should have made her strong. Shouldn't we? Or at least protected her. Surely one life, made happy, is worth more than all the philosophy, all the theorising in the world? If it is our calling, to help in the advancement of mankind, surely we must acknowledge what it is to be human? And if that means sensitivity, or weakness, or rashness, then so be it. People are not gods. And there is nothing to be gained in trying to make them so.

GODWIN. I cannot agree with you.

MARY. No. I don't suppose you can.

GODWIN. That is an apology for complacency. For indolence.
For stupification…

MARY. Why can our humanity not be our strength?

GODWIN. We must seek to analyse the frailties of our nature,
and then to reach beyond them…

MARY. I think that is a dangerous philosophy.

Pause.

GODWIN. It is a privilege – to be amongst the legislators of
mankind. And you will be, Mary. As your mother was, as I
am. And as Shelley will be too.

We are keeping him waiting.

MARY. Yes.

GODWIN. If I were going to lose you to anyone, it were best to
him. I see that now.

MARY. You haven't lost me.

GODWIN. Come then. Society demands its pound of flesh.

*He holds out his hand to her. She goes to him and puts her
hand in his. He hugs her suddenly.*

A privilege.

They leave.

End.

Afterword

This play began with a question: how did Mary Shelley, aged only eighteen, come to write a novel of such weight and power as *Frankenstein*? I knew the story of the Villa Diodati, and the external impetus for her sitting down to write, but where did the thoughts come from? The themes? For *Frankenstein* is clearly more than a spine-chiller; it is a novel of ideas.

She dedicated the story to her father, William Godwin, the radical political philosopher. Much has been said about Shelley's influence on Mary at this time (some have even suggested that he had a hand in writing *Frankenstein*), but as I began my research, I quickly discovered that Shelley's own ideas and preoccupations had been inspired to a large degree by Godwinian philosophy. He and Mary shared a passion for her father's work, and I started to understand that it was this passion more than anything that had equipped her to write so brilliantly about such ideas as the consequences of treating men like beasts.

But there was more. Mary was writing *Frankenstein* at a time when her relationship with her father was under great strain – when he had refused all contact with her for almost two years. The novel is more than a homage to his philosophies; it is a criticism of his nature and his choices, a warning, a reprimand and a huge cry for understanding. It is these elements, I think, that give *Frankenstein* its heartfelt urgency and power. I decided to place this complex relationship at the centre of the play, and to see where it took me.

The research I undertook was enormously absorbing and inspiring. Each of the principal characters could be the subject of a play in their own right. I loved delving into Skinner Street – into Mary's troubled family, patched together from bits and pieces of different relationships, crudely stitched – like the monster himself – into a clumsy, dysfunctional form. I loved discovering her sisters, each of whose fate was so bound up

A Nick Hern Book

Mary Shelley first published in Great Britain as a paperback original in 2012 by Nick Hern Books Limited, 14 Larden Road, London W3 7ST, in association with Shared Experience, Nottingham Playhouse and West Yorkshire Playhouse

Mary Shelley copyright © 2012 Helen Edmundson

Helen Edmundson has asserted her right to be identified as the author of this work

Cover photograph by Robert Day with Kristin Atherton as Mary Shelley
Cover design by Ned Hoste, 2H

Typeset by Nick Hern Books, London
Printed in the UK by CPI Group (UK) Ltd, Croydon, CR0 4YY

A CIP catalogue record for this book is available from the British Library

ISBN 978 1 84842 257 5

with Mary's, and learning about the daring and vision of Shelley's early socialism. It was a pleasure to imagine these people back to life.

And whilst I felt compelled (as Mary did) to depict the very real and awful dangers of putting principles before emotional need, I hope I have not painted too harsh a picture of idealism. For there is something courageous, surely, in striving to break new ground in the perilous business of living. In deciding to deal with the pain, the guilt, the disapproval this entails, in the belief and hope that, ultimately, humanity will be the richer for your efforts.

Helen Edmundson
February 2012